By Heart:
THE ART OF MEMORIZING MUSIC

By Heart:
THE ART OF MEMORIZING MUSIC

Paul Cienniwa, DMA

With a foreword by Larry Thomas Bell, FAAR

Copyright © 2014 Paul Cienniwa
All rights reserved.
ISBN: 1496180690
ISBN-13: 978-1496180698

for Jacqueline

Memory is the scribe of the soul.

—Aristotle

Contents

Foreword	xiii
Acknowledgments	xvii
Introduction	1

Why Bother?

To Memorize or Not to Memorize	3
My Story	3
Not an Easy Path	4
Why Should You Memorize?	5
Why *Shouldn't* You Memorize?	8
We Owe It	10

The Early Stages of Memorization

Getting Started	13
Ground Rules	14
Three Types of Memory	16
The Practice Log	18
Online Practice Log	19
A Timer	20
You and Your Metronome	22
Those Good Habits	24
At What Stage?	24
Landmarks	26
You Say Memory, I Say Mnemonic	28
A Discernible Regularity	30
But Wait ... There's More!	32

Developing Aural Memory	34
Working Away from the Instrument	35
Those Slow Pieces	37
Daily Routine, with Variety	38
Knowing When to Take Time off	40
Taking an Old Friend to Heart	41
Now You're Dancing on Air!	42
Touching the Void	43

THE MIDDLE STAGE OF MEMORIZATION

You've Got It! … (or so You Think)	45
Respect!	46
Mental Techniques	47
Playing Techniques	48
Trap Doors	51
Are We There Yet?	52
Practice Performances	53

A FEW STICKING POINTS

Fear Factor	55
Tales of Fear!	56
The Inner Game	57
Total Presence	58
A Meditation	60
Improvisation	61

THE MEMORIZED RECITAL

It's Recital Time!	63
Now Stop Practicing!	64
Practicing for Performance	66
More Mental Work	68
Practice Performances Redux	69
Hanging out Backstage	71
Stage Presence	72
The Importance of a Clear Mind	73
Resuscitating a Program	74

CONCLUSIONS

A Summary of How	77
Postscript	78

APPENDIX I
   Dear Harpsichordists, Why Don't We
   Play from Memory?   81

APPENDIX II
   A Checklist for Memorizing a New Piece   86

APPENDIX III
   A Checklist for the Memorized Program   88

INDEX   91

Foreword
by Larry Thomas Bell, FAAR

In the 1840s pianists Clara Schumann and Franz Liszt started playing public recitals from memory. The lid was opened and the piano moved so the soundboard would face the audience. (More importantly, so the audience could admire Liszt's distinguished profile.) Thus begins the modern recital, as well as its consequent litany of liabilities that Paul Cienniwa describes in his monograph of musical memory.

What does music have to do with memory? Composers, writers, poets, and playwrights all seem to find inspiration (or substance) in their first memories of life. Composers have memories of our earliest glimpses of gesture and movement, the ultimate basis of all musical composition (which is, surprisingly, not necessarily sound). This explains why there are no real compositional prodigies, as opposed to performing prodigies. Mozart, Saint-Saëns, and Mendelssohn, each considered prodigious, did not write anything of substance before age sixteen. Composers must have some basis of experience from which to write. Only age can provide that.

On the one hand is the somewhat abstract business of musical memory and on the other the more practical business of memorizing a given piece of music. Paul Cienniwa enthusiastically takes on the problems of the later. He begins with his own ability to sight-read fluently. Largely taken for granted, this ability should not be: a good sight-reader has already assimilated musical notation in his mind.

I have had the privilege to work with some of the great sight-readers of music. Percussionist Zita Carno could sight-read the most complex scores (often with three or four staff lines), pan-chromatic, polyrhythmic, and densely polyphonic. When asked, "How do you sight-read?" she would say, in a thick Bronx accent, "What I don't read I memorize, darling."

During my Rome Prize year (1982-83) I resumed my concert career as a pianist. I wrote to my composition teacher Vincent Persichetti, also a pianist, to ask how he memorized. He responded, "I put the score up in my mind and read it." Persichetti, whose savant-like memory of the Western canon of music was legendary, seemed also to begin with an equally astonishing ability to read at sight.

Equally impressive was Roger Sessions's total recall (in his eighties) of the entire prelude to *Tristan und Isolde* demonstrated by writing it out on the wall-length blackboard in his classroom at The Juilliard School. He could also play by heart Beethoven's original sketches for the finale of the Op. 132 string quartet and the original instrumental finale of the Ninth Symphony.

Anyone who has witnessed phenomenal feats of musical memory asks, "How is this being done?" Cognitive science tells us we can only remember simultaneously seven discrete things. Music would appear to contain many more than seven. Upon closer examination of almost any celebrated masterpiece, however, one usually finds an elaboration of one or two unique patterns covering the entire piece. Through analysis (best done away from an instrument) one can discover these examples of varied repetition, characteristic fingerprints of the work. This is only a starting point, but it does explain how someone like Yo-Yo Ma (not to take anything away from his achievement) can play all six Bach 'cello suites from memory on a given day. Each suite has its own set of unique motivic shapes that are continuously varied. These shapes can be gleaned through a thorough study of theory, ear-training, analysis, and music history.

To give one short example from the keyboard repertoire of motivic elaboration: the first six notes—a descending scale from G to B^b—is the basis for Mozart's Sonata in B^b Major, K. 333. All of the thematic material for each of the three movements is based on this one ordinary shape. In addition, each measure of the piece contains some element of this basic shape. In composers such as Beethoven, whose music is even more thematically concentrated, this is even more often the case.

Finally something has to be said about the way we retain music by ear. The knowledge I obtained in the years spent with Madame Renée Longy, saturated with every aspect of solfège technique, has become the lasting basis of my life as a musician. Not only did she teach us all how to assimilate musical notation thoroughly and fluently, but she also taught us to trust our pitch sense and that nothing was more important than the articulation of the phrase.

Paul Cienniwa offers us a fresh look inside the world of the practicing musician. Not only does he attempt to come to terms with how he memorizes music and give the reader concrete practices to follow, but his enthusiasm demonstrates that the real basis of learning is the *joy of work*.

Acknowledgments

Thank you to Michael Ruiz, my conservatory piano teacher who provided the foundation for my memorization practice.

Thank you to my house concert audiences who graciously allow me to try out newly memorized repertoire. Thank you as well to Jackie for always throwing a great reception.

Thank you to my public audiences over the past four years who never expected anything but memorized repertoire.

Thank you to the audience members and musician colleagues who, in asking how I memorize, inspired me to write this book.

Thank you to my blog readers who offered comments throughout the blog writing process.

Thank you to my good friend Karl Henning and my mother Marilyn Majewski for reading and commenting on the manuscript.

Thank you to Larry Thomas Bell for writing the Foreword and for constant encouragement.

Above all, thank you to Andrea Olmstead for encouraging me to reconsider my writing, again and again.

Introduction

In 2010 I decided to return to playing from memory after about eighteen years of playing from score. Since that return, musician colleagues and audience members have asked exactly how I memorize music. After much contemplation, I decided to create a blog to discuss publicly my process of memorization. That blog and the many good comments from my readers led to the book you are now reading.

This book is primarily an exploration of *how* one can memorize music. Since it is my own process, I like to think it is also how one *should* memorize. I am not so naive as to suggest there is only one way to memorize music, but I would like to posit that my approach creates as solid a foundation as possible. That foundation will help you to avoid memory slips in concert and ensure better retention in the long run. It will make recovering a piece after years away from it much quicker, and it will maximize the efficiency of your practice time.

This is not a scholarly book. It is all opinion based on my own experiences. Although I refer to several texts and websites throughout the book, I don't intend for the reader to take every word as documented fact. You are your own person, and you experience life in your own way, just as I experience life in my own way. I hope that my experiences in memorization will assist you in reaching your own memorization goals.

If you are new to memorization, this book will give you the skills and techniques to get started with the process. You will carry those skills and techniques for the rest of your life. Even if you already have a solid memorization practice, this book can inspire some new or different approaches while also reinforcing your own convictions.

When I was writing the blog, a number of readers commented that many of the techniques I presented were good for any type of practice, even for one not working towards memorization. That said, this book is also a useful foundational study of how to practice.

This book may not be terribly long, but don't let that fool you into thinking good memorization is a short process. It takes time, patience, and self-motivation. It is not easy, but it will become easier over time. Musical memorization is a lot of work, but the rewards are really, really great.

Are you ready to work? Let's memorize!

Why Bother?

To Memorize or Not to Memorize

Why do musicians choose to memorize—or not memorize—music? Is there any decision-making at all, or are musicians merely stuck in a tradition? What if you were confident enough as a musician to make up your own mind?

In my case, I started out as a pianist, and I never thought twice about memorizing. It simply is what one *does*. But then I put myself into a rather different position by deciding to become a harpsichordist. In doing so, I entered a modern tradition that doesn't require memorization.

If you are reading this book, you most likely already feel that you should memorize your music. If you feel otherwise, I may not be able to persuade you to memorize. Whichever the case, it is important to consider why you should or should not memorize.

My Story

I started playing the piano when I was six, and for as long as I played, memorization was required. By the time I entered conservatory at seventeen, memorization was an expected skill, although, that early on, I didn't have much grasp of how I was doing it.

In 1992, when I switched from being a "piano major" to a "harpsichord major," I no longer had to memorize. My piano teacher, while very disappointed I wasn't going to pursue the piano any more, seemed even more upset that I was going to lose the memorization techniques we had worked so hard to build.

In 2010 and after years of contemplation, I decided to return to playing from memory. Thus, I gave up memorization when I was twenty, and I came back to it at age thirty-eight.

This has given me a unique perspective. When I started trying to memorize nearly twenty years later, I was amazed by the differences from so many years earlier. For instance:
- my ear was much, much better
- I understood musical form
- I had a firm grasp of harmony and compositional practices
- I had an infinitely better technique
- I had far more confidence as a musician
- very importantly, I had about twenty years of performing under my belt

You know that fantasy of being able to go back to elementary or high school with the brain and wisdom of an adult? This was a little bit like that.

This is *not at all* to imply, however, that it has been an easy path.

Not an Easy Path

My very first back-to-memory experiences weren't good ones. I had significant memory slips. In the first two experiences in which I played the same binary-form Bach movement, the memory slips were so severe I had to noodle my way through the B section to a final cadence. I don't even think that my ending key was the same as the starting key.

I should have known better. Indeed, my return-to-memory work had consisted mainly of repetition. Then again, this was more or less how I had been practicing when I worked *with* music.

I continued to have slips, and I *continue* to have slips, but the nature of today's memory slips is not the same and, most importantly, the recovery is quite different. While it is possible that a few individuals are capable of playing note-perfect, memorized programs, I am convinced that the majority of memorized recitals have a fair share of near-misses and faking. This is not to suggest that we should strive towards imperfection, but we need to work as inhabitants of an imperfect world.

As you now know, I skipped nearly twenty years of playing from memory. With that perspective comes confidence as a player. Perhaps this confidence has kept me from the fear that most people would have with on-stage memory slips, but I am not so sure. I would like to suggest that, in order to conquer memory-related fear, we must both accept that perfection is, while desired, nearly impossible and always have an exit strategy.

Before continuing, I want to make something very clear: I don't believe that I have any special gift for memorization. This has been *hard work*, and it continues to be *hard work*. I started writing about my memorization process because I think that the difficulties I have had are probably some of the same difficulties others have experienced. With this empathetic understanding, we can all become better at learning music by heart and, in turn, become better musicians.

Why Should You Memorize?

In 2010, shortly after I made my firm commitment to play from memory, I wrote an article geared towards harpsichordists titled, "Dear Harpsichordists, Why Don't We Play from Memory?" (The full article appears in Appendix I.) I have learned much since writing that article, although many of my comments still ring true today.

In the article, I stated that the main reason I returned to memorization practice was that I had felt that, by playing with music, I had never truly learned my programs. I then highlighted a few of the pleasant results that come with working from memory:
- lighting is no longer problematic
- page turns are no longer an issue

- I make better repertoire choices (that is, having to commit something to memory makes one think a lot harder about what one decides to learn)
- phrasing is better, and interpretations are more personal

After the article was published, harpsichord builder Allan Winkler pointed out that I should have said that I could *hear* the instrument better without the music desk blocking the sound. He is absolutely right.

All of these comments were true then, and they are still true for me today. Since then, I have observed a few more advantages that come with working from memory:

- My technique is more solid. Memory practice requires repetition—usually *slow* repetition—and this ensures greater accuracy.
- I can travel more lightly. Of course, I always bring scores to performances, but it is nice to be able to think through my scores on the beach, on the plane, while trying to sleep … anywhere!
- I am much more aware of intonation issues. As a harpsichordist, I am always aware of tuning issues, but now I hear them better. More so, I can address them: without the music desk in place, I can tune *when* I need to and with little trouble. Regardless of instrument, I am sure that playing from memory makes one much more aware of one's intonation and the intonation of others.
- This should go without saying: I know my music better. I have quite a few anecdotes about how poorly I knew my music pre-memory. In short, playing from score *forces* the acknowledgment and comprehension of key elements of the musical process, such as phrase length.
- I wasn't aware of this before returning to memory, but now, if I practice with music for a long time, I notice some back and neck pain. I suggest that playing without score puts one into a more natural posture. Indeed, it is more ergonomic.
- I have pride of ownership. How nice it is to go to an instrument and play by heart! The music has become *my* music.

- Finally, this has been a shot in the arm for my mid-career (if being in one's 40's is mid-career). It is easy to get bogged down in wondering what one should practice, how much, how little, and even why. Having memorization as a goal removes the existentialism from the practice room, and it puts one's work into laser-sharp focus.

Aside from creating those general ideas about the benefits of playing from memory, my return to memorization practice did something for me that was completely unexpected:

Practicing—with the goal of playing recitals by heart—forced me to recall and follow all of the good things my best teachers taught me.

In other words, playing from memory forces good habits.

I quickly learned that, if I don't follow those good habits, I will fall flat on my face in performance. Likewise, *not* playing from memory for so many years had allowed me to become apathetic in the practice room.

So what were these good habits that resurfaced?
- written/consistent fingering
- using a metronome
- slow practice
- creating a practice log/journal
- studying the score away from the instrument
- playing programs for others *before* making public appearances

I did all of these things (more or less) when I practiced to perform from score. But playing from memory has made them essential, indeed, *mandatory*.

Why *Shouldn't* You Memorize?

I think there are some very good reasons why and when one shouldn't perform from memory. First, there really isn't a solid tradition of performing ensemble music from memory. One might consider concertos, but, then again, the orchestra isn't playing from memory. There exists, interestingly, a newer tradition of some classical ensembles, particularly in the early music world, performing from memory, but these seem to be anomalies. In some choral singing there is a memorized tradition, particularly among children's choirs. The Philippine Madrigal Singers, a top-notch adult ensemble, perform from memory—and, I should add, seated and without a conductor.

Because one plays chamber music with a variety of people, often playing the same pieces with different ensembles, playing without music would be quite disadvantageous. I am not suggesting that a memorized piece is a "learned" performance of that piece, but, in chamber music, we often need to mark up our parts as interpretive decisions are made. Keeping track of all of those decisions would be difficult and could be disastrous in performance, without even considering score-based memory slips. Memorizing chamber music is not impossible, but, for me, memory work takes a lot of my time, and I am not at the point in my career or interest where I want to devote that much time to my ensemble players. Were I a string player in a permanent string quartet, however, I think that playing the great quartet repertoire from memory with excellent colleagues would be wonderful.

Contemporary music is quite commonly performed from score. Not only is new repertoire often hot off the press with composers revising until the last minute, non-tonal music can also be wickedly difficult to commit to memory. In addition, some contemporary composers don't expect their music to be played by heart.

> Composer Larry Bell, who wrote the Foreword to this book, shared this anecdote with me:
>
>> There is a book by (the late) Charles Rosen about Elliott Carter's piano music. At the time the book was written, Mr. Carter had not written very much piano music, so the book is a thin one and fundamentally about the one and only Piano Sonata (1945-6).
>>
>> At any rate, even in the 1950's Carter had a reputation as a composer who wrote difficult music. Rosen, showing himself to be a progressive pianist, took on the Carter Sonata and played it many, many times from memory.
>>
>> Once, when in the wings of Coolidge Auditorium at the Library of Congress waiting to go on stage to play the Carter, a stagehand asked Mr. Rosen what piece it was that he was about to play. When Rosen replied the 'Carter Sonata,' the stage hand said, 'Oh, that is a very difficult work.'
>>
>> The concert was somewhat of a disaster, and from that time onwards Rosen was never again able to play the Carter Sonata from memory.

While this list of reasons why one shouldn't memorize is far from complete, I will leave this final suggestion: One should not play from memory if the piece isn't learned well enough. Let's face it, we are all busy people, and we simply may not have enough time to commit a piece to memory. But this should not be the norm. We need to make more time for our practice, *even if it means that we will be performing a little less often.*

And, as I have already suggested, working towards memory isn't just about the audience, but also about our own musical development.

We Owe It

I have now listed some of my reasons as to *why* one should perform music by heart. But the most important one remains:

We owe it to the music we love.

We owe it to the music we love because memorized music is better-learned music. By memorizing music, we are not obstructed by physical objects such as pages and lighting. We attain a more solid technique through the process of memorization. We develop a better conception of a composer's sense of form, phrase, and harmony. We become more disciplined in our own practice because of the demands of memorization.

We owe it to the music we love because a performance of memorized music engages the audience more. We choose only the best repertoire to commit to memory. We appear before an audience only when we know the music is ready to be played. We create convincing and well-conceived interpretations through the process of memorization.

I could go on and on with this litany!

Even if you don't believe that memorized music is better-learned music, it is hard to argue that playing from score is more engaging for the audience. It is just as hard to argue that there's no difference for an audience.

And this comes to my final point. Is classical music dying? Maybe it is, maybe not. One can hardly argue that classical music is healthy or that audiences are impatient to hear the next recital.

Think about it, classical musicians. We don't have audiences screaming for our music, and we have been fighting a tide of pop culture for a long time. We need to do everything we can to bring in and retain our audiences. While memorization is only a piece of the puzzle, I can't imagine that audiences—*especially* new audiences—want to watch us *read* music when they have taken the time and money to sit down and quietly listen to us. We owe it to our audiences and the repertoire we love to give our best, and this includes working ten times harder to play music convincingly without a score.

It is time to do something about this. And now it is time for *how*.

The Early Stages Of Memorization

Getting Started

When I returned to work from memory, I had to make some strategic decisions. How in the world was I going to do it? I already had some engagements, and I couldn't just memorize a recital in a few months after being away from the process for so many years.

My initial thought was to learn a piece by heart and then play it on a program in which I would play everything else with music. How would the listener perceive this? Would it seem pretentious to pull away the music for a "special" piece? Would it then be confusing to go back to the score for the rest of the program?

My solution was to play a short Bach work from memory on a program of otherwise non-memorized contemporary music. It didn't work out too well, and I suffered several memory slips. I quickly learned that my "memory brain" differed palpably from my "reading music brain." How so? Each type of brain use seems to work different neurons.

I don't give up too easily, so I started to explore other avenues. My first decision was to not think too hard about when I was going to perform. This decision can be described in one simple word: *patience*. Even today I regularly return to that one word. One cannot memorize well hastily and impatiently. Since you are going through the trouble of memorization, you might as well do it slowly and carefully so that it sticks. Patience.

My next decision was to think hard about repertoire. I started small, with short works. As I quickly learned, plenty of short works by Bach are difficult to memorize, so I decided to work on other composers while also choosing forms that I thought would be fairly simple:
- rondo (*rondeau*), also known as refrain forms
- binary
- theme and variation

I settled on the large *Passacaille* in C Major by Louis Couperin. This beautiful but simple *rondeau* has a short, catchy refrain and a series of episodes (*couplets*) that last only about eight bars each. I knew, quite simply, that if I were to have a memory slip in concert, I would be able to get back to that refrain and then move on to the next *couplet* with ease. Best of all, the *rondeau* had a lot of *couplets*, making it a relatively long piece. Once I got the whole thing going, I had nearly seven minutes of music.

From that *rondeau* came another Louis Couperin *rondeau*: the *Chaconne ou Passacaille* in G Minor. Now I had twelve minutes of music. Then a miracle happened: I was asked to prepare some recitals with a recorder-playing colleague. The recital wouldn't only consist of recorder and harpsichord ensemble music, so I would have a chance to play my newly memorized solo pieces. And I did, to great success each time.

(You might wonder how I moved from "reading music brain" to "memory brain" in these performances. It wasn't that hard, especially since it felt more like moving from "accompanying brain" to "memory brain." I wasn't playing any solo repertoire with music, and that made all the difference.)

Ground Rules

In time, I established a few ground rules for my memorization work, and I still follow those rules today:

Program planning is of utmost importance. Memorization takes time, a lot of work, and plenty of maintenance. I have to be extremely careful to choose works I will want to play for the rest of my life. Life is short, so why devote it to B-list composers or compositions? Why make your audience hear anything but the best? Some audience members don't need to hear Bach's Italian Concerto again, but it is a useful piece for any keyboardist to have in his or her repertoire—as well as an excellent piece of music. Without getting too much into how to build a program, just consider that every piece you commit to memory should be something you will play for more than one season. If not, is it really worth your time?

In that same vein and as one who returned to memory after years of playing from score, I focus at least 50% of my time on works I have already played. Why reinvent the wheel? If I have already performed A-list works successfully years ago with music, why not make them part of my permanent memory? This approach helped me to build some repertoire immediately. In most cases, I have been able to memorize the previously learned (but not memorized) music in less than half the time of new works. I try to keep a healthy mix of old and new repertoire, with the purpose of committing everything to memory.

I have a big gap in the concerto repertoire, so I have also made learning one concerto at a time a top priority. Oh, sure, I have concerto repertoire … but now I need to memorize it. In conservatory, we musicians are always forced to learn concertos with, quite possibly, little hope of ever playing them in front of an orchestra. What if that opportunity arises? One never knows, and it would be a real shame to turn down a good opportunity.

Patience is extremely important when developing a solid memory. For this reason, I insist on working pieces in different stages of development. Starting everything from scratch at the same time is deadly to one's patience, focus, and motivation. I shall go into more detail later when I discuss the use of a practice log and a timer, but, to start, a typical practice session for me might include these types of pieces:
- brand new work (30')
- review of almost-completed work (20')
- half-learned concerto movement (40')

- review of ready-to-go work (15')
- start memorizing previously learned work (30')

Note that the "ready-to-go work" takes the least amount of my practice time.

Finally, because memorized repertoire *is* permanent repertoire, review what you have spent so much time to learn. Although probably impossible to keep everything fresh, it would be a tragedy to let your work wither on the vine. Can one keep a full program ready all the time while learning another program? Maybe—although I don't have enough practice time in the day. It should be possible to keep a half program alive, however. Since "ready-to-go" pieces take less time to practice, why not play fifteen minutes of concert repertoire each day? Keep it ready, keep it fresh. Your audience needs you!

Whether you are working on memorization daily, getting back to memorization, or starting for the first time, remember *patience*. Know your *limits* and to build your practice time to be useful, relevant, and not so taxing that you have trouble resuming the next day. *Plan your time well.* And, above all, one piece is a good start.

Three Types of Memory

Quite a bit of information about musical memory exists on the internet. I find it, however, either too scientific or too cursory. The scientific pages go into great detail about what might be going on in the brain, while other sites tend to give a series of tips in short form. Because memorization is such an intense, drawn-out process, I find that a handful of tips don't do justice to the needs of the process. In turn, scientific research doesn't create an applied, practical approach.

While there is some variation among the research, three main types of memory are generally accepted:
- tactile
- aural
- visual

Some of the research adds extra categories, such as structural, emotional, and linguistic, but I think that these are subcategories or crossover categories from the three main types. (For more on these categories, see Chapter 33 in the *Oxford Handbook of Musical Psychology*, Oxford University Press, 2008.)

Tactile memory, generally considered the most fleeting, is the memory of automatic response. As muscle memory, it has little, if any, basis in the intellect and is learned by simple repetition. On the whole, tactile memory comes into play with extremely technical music. While it is often the first type of memory to be lost under pressure, it has also saved me in a number of instances when I couldn't see or hear what was coming next. Thankfully, my fingers kept on going.

Aural memory is best when a musician has an excellent ear—and one can never have too good an ear. While one may lose tactile memory, aural ability allows one to play by ear, anticipating upcoming pitches by "hearing" and finding those notes in advance. The memorization process will be greatly accelerated when one has already heard a piece many times, either by playing it oneself or by hearing other performances. For this reason, memorizing a piece from scratch without having previously heard it can be a lengthy process.

Visual memory is self-explanatory: seeing the music as you are playing it. This type of memory can be built entirely at the instrument but is most solid when learned away from the instrument. To be clear, this doesn't necessarily mean that you are seeing each note as it appears on the page. Although that is possible for some, most people have an abstract representation in their mind's eye. When I have a program ready to play, I will spend at least half, if not two-thirds, of my time away from the instrument, visualizing the score in "mental" practice.

This leaves us with those subcategories. All three mentioned (structural, emotional, and linguistic) are created when practicing the main types of memory. Structural is based in musical form, and it needs to be tied to all three memory types from the beginning of the process. Emotional memory might have more to do with performance experience and even anxiety. In my opinion, it doesn't hold a solid place in the practice room, although one must learn to manage and be aware of this type of memory. Finally, linguistic memory—the process of narratively guiding oneself through various cues and landmarks—is also one of the three main types of memory. Based in cues and landmarks, it is closely tied to structural memory and, by association, the three main memory types.

This is about as scientific as this book will get, and I am not nearly as scientific as the hardcore research out there. If I could summarize the goal of my approach to memorization, it would be this:

I should be able to write out every memorized piece away from the instrument.

To do so, I will call upon my visual, my aural, and even my tactile memory.

The Practice Log

I cannot stress enough the importance of good planning and good record keeping. As a diary of your daily work, your practice log lists what you accomplished in your previous session and what you hope to accomplish in the current and future sessions. Use your log to list your goals, problem areas, successes, needs—anything that comes to mind when practicing. (I even use my log to jot down fleeting thoughts that might enter while practicing. Need to buy milk? Write it down quickly, and get that distracting thought out of your head!)

Your practice log will list metronome markings, timings, thoughts on musical form, emotions about the music—whatever you feel your practice session needs or will require in the future. If you take a few days away from practice, you will find that the log helps remind you of where you have been and what you need to do.

Each day, before practicing, map out your practice session:
- How much time do you have?
- How will you divide your time?
- Based on yesterday's log, what needs to be addressed today?

Some days the entries are short, others long. You might use spare pages to create a chart of metronome markings with your intended tempo goals and the steps you have been taking to reach them. In these cases, I flip back to these charts and update them each day. When I have a full program to prepare, I create a check-off list indicating the movements I have played at the instrument and those movements I have worked on away from the instrument.

Over the years, I have saved my practice logs. Not only do they make nice keepsakes of hard work, you can also refer to them years later when revisiting some old repertoire.

Now go out and splurge for a nice notebook. You might be keeping it for a long time!

Online Practice Log

My conservatory piano teacher Michael Ruiz used to say that he wanted to own a Victorian house where all of his students would live. I suppose this meant that he would be available for coaching at any time and that all of the students would improve through semi-supervised hard work and osmosis.

He would also talk about a scenario in which one student would practice while another would observe. The logic here was that the practicing student would be forced to be honest and more diligent about using the practice time wisely. The observing student would learn from the practicing student's actions.

When I started the blog as a foundation for this book, I became increasingly aware that my own work had improved as I put forth my ideas behind memorization practice. In effect, the blog became Ruiz's idealized practice room, with me as the practicing student and the internet readers as the observers.

> While I was writing the blog, I thought it would be useful to me, and possibly to other readers, to post my daily practice log to the internet. Not only did the discipline assure that I would use my practice log more regularly (yes, there have been gaps), it assured that I would be thinking even harder about what I was doing each time I practiced. It became a lab/practicum to the blog, and I posted it regularly to Twitter and Facebook.
>
> Give it a try! You might not be able to live in a Victorian house with your fellow musicians, but the internet can become your practice room.

A Timer

The next step to making your practice focused, efficient, and patient is to use a timer. I time every bit of my practice. Call me compulsive, but I even time my breaks. (For the record, I wrote this book during breaks from the instrument.)

The timer works at both ends of the practice spectrum: it moderates the exciting moments, when one wants to keep on working while avoiding everything else, and it forces those moments when one might not be so motivated. Let's begin by looking at one end of the spectrum.

When you are excited about a piece, it is easy to continue on and on. Then you ignore all of the other things on your plate, and, before you know it, all of your practice time is gone for the day. For me, the worst thing is when I practice one piece so much that I don't feel like practicing it the next day—or anything else the next day. To this end, the timer keeps everything in moderation.

Let's face it: memorization practice (or any practice, really) is hard work. It is not always fun, and one can get distracted by email, phone calls, or writing a book about memorization. *The timer keeps limits while also making obligations.*

It is important to know, before beginning the practice session, how much time you have. From there, divide up your time. Don't forget breaks. Use a time log, and stick to it. (You can always change it the next day.) If you are doing this for the first time, my advice is to work with shorter time frames. You will be pleasantly surprised to see how much you can accomplish in a short amount of *focused* time. If you have a smartphone, you probably have a timer with your clock app. (You may also have a stopwatch with that app—another important tool.) A kitchen timer is a low-tech option as well. Set the timer and obey it.

A timer helps you know your limits. It forces patience, encouraging you to do a little each day instead of too much one day and nothing the next. As Aesop wrote of the tortoise and the hare, "Slow and steady wins the race."

I haven't written yet about how exactly to memorize notes, but repetition is a large part of the process. Repetition practice can be redundant, and redundancy results in thoughtless and inattentive practice. With a timer, one can address the need for thoughtful repetition practice while avoiding spending too much time in redundant practice.

In a typical day, I try to practice about three hours. I might start first thing in the morning with two thirty-minute sessions and then a thirty-minute break. Because I am most creative in the morning, I really need to set a timer during my breaks. Otherwise it is easy to get caught up in break activity. And since break activity is often at the computer, it becomes extremely easy to lose a sense of time.

Until I started using a timer regularly, I simply couldn't practice in the afternoon due to inattentiveness and lack of motivation. Knowing this, I would squeeze everything in before lunch, with short breaks and a mad dash to the finish. But the timer has helped me to pace my work better, and, with short practice blocks, I can now easily continue into the afternoon.

Regardless of how much or how little time you have, a timer will help you to function either within a completely open-ended day or during a busy day, when you have to spend most of it at your day job. Whichever your case may be, a timer is the best solution for disciplined practice.

You and Your Metronome

Much of what I can say about using a metronome is standard wisdom for those who practice music. Even if you doubt the musicality of the metronome, knowing where the absolute beat should lie is highly useful information.

For the memorizing musician, the metronome assumes a new significance. Because we are working without score and, sometimes in performance, under fear of a memory slip, it is good to know the optimal tempo for a piece. By optimal, I don't mean "fastest." When one works from memory, one can easily become too concerned with the notes or the maintenance of memory to give much thought to tempo. Of course, this scenario would indicate that one isn't completely listening to what one is doing—but that is another matter entirely. Suffice it to say one should know how fast or how slow a piece ought to go. This is your own interpretive decision, unless the composer has left specific indications.

I have a hunch that musicians who don't play from memory also don't do much metronome work. As I think working from memory forces all good habits, I am aware that *not* working from memory allows for apathy. In my own case, I didn't use a metronome for years. When I started working with living composers, knowing their tempo became a necessity; when I started working from memory, knowing *my* own tempo became even more imperative.

When I resumed my memory work, I didn't start working with a metronome immediately. Only when I arrived to do my warmup at one concert did I realize that almost all of my fast tempi were identical. That is disconcerting to realize right before a recital! My only explanation is that, in my memorization work, I had settled into a comfortable pace with tempi and had not really thought much about it until I was on the spot. I submit that, had I not been playing that recital from memory, I might never have noticed it at all. Memory forces a certain level of self-examination.

My own anecdotes aside, there are specific ways metronome work can help your memorization practice.

1. Slow metronome work (from memory, of course) helps to avoid any reliance on tactile memory.
2. Slow metronome work helps to avoid sentimental practice. It is easy to get caught up in the emotions of our music. By forcing a slow tempo, we can focus just on making sure that we know the notes.
3. Slow metronome work makes sure that a piece is rock-solid. Every note goes in its precise metric place, and this ensures that every note is properly memorized.

As you can see, I don't have much use for *a tempo* metronome work, except when I am trying to find the optimal tempo for a piece. From the standpoint of learning memorization, a metronome set well below optimal tempo is the best tool.

I haven't written too much yet about working away from the instrument, but a favorite technique is to work with a metronome set at a slow tempo. The metronome is excellent at keeping my mind from wandering while mentally working my way through a score. It keeps me from rushing my mind through my well-memorized passages, and, just as when playing, it makes sure that every note is sitting in its correct metric place.

Those Good Habits

Much of what I have already discussed should provide some fairly redundant information for anyone with a good practice discipline. The use of a practice log, metronome, and timer are standard tools for many, if not most, successful musicians. They are mentioned in the context of this book on memorization practice because, as it was in my case, *not* memorizing for so many years helped me to neglect some of those good habits long ago learned.

That is not to say that I wasn't using a metronome, practice log, or timer over the years, but it is to say that committing to memorization practice has made those items essential. Returning to memory forced those good habits to return.

None of the information so far has, in fact, told the reader how to memorize specific notes. As we will soon see, there isn't one way, and the memorization process will include multiple components, just as there are three, and possibly more, types of memory.

Because the memorization process is multifaceted, it is best to have as much as possible working for you, and this includes using all of the good habits that you may have already learned. So, take a moment to consider what your good habits are now and what they may have been at one time. If you haven't been using them, isn't it time to start again?

At What Stage?

When should you start memorizing a piece? A lot of people think you should "learn" it first and commit it to memory later. If you have already performed a piece with music, it is certainly easier to memorize it later on than totally from scratch.

But at its core, "learning" a piece with music before memorizing the piece is a flawed approach. Why? Because one will surely develop a tactile memory before aural or visual memory are established. As I have already written, tactile memory is the least reliable form of memory.

Let's play devil's advocate. What are the advantages of bringing a piece to playing level and *then* memorizing it?
- **Tactile Advantage**: The piece is in your fingers, now you just have to commit it to memory.
- **Aural Advantage**: You've played the piece a lot from score—so much that you've brought it to performance level. Now it's in your ears.
- **Visual Advantage**: You've seen the score so many times that you have been able to solidify tactile and aural memory. It shouldn't be hard to visualize the score away from the instrument.

Wow! These are really strong advantages, and, as I write this, I am wondering if I should take up this method.

Let's look at those three advantages carefully. Presuming you take my advice to heart, you will see that "learning" a piece and then memorizing it becomes a two-step process. You have taken a lot of time to get a piece up to playing level, and now you have to go back to a crawl in order to bring it to a non-tactile-based memory level. Unfortunately, your foundation will always be one of tactile memory since that is what sticks before aural and visual memory become certain.

In the end, it may seem that the "play first" method is faster. Aside from it being a two-step process, however, it has the potential of also creating an insecure foundation in tactile memory. Just as correcting wrong notes is very difficult when you have already learned them as right notes, undoing tactile memory to create an aural/intellectual foundation will take much time. Even once you are good to go, you may still have concerns about your shaky starting foundation. Take it from one who knows: practice patience.

In my own work, I never "learn" a piece before committing it to memory. I am a very good sight-reader, so, unfortunately, it is easy for me to get a piece to a reasonable state in very little time. My goal is to completely know a piece, however, and I firmly believe that this is only possible with *true* memorization.

> What is "true" memorization? It is the real deal, not the kind that non-memorizers talk about ... you know, the "oh, yeah, it's practically memorized" types of musicians. These musicians resemble those people who say that they understand and read a foreign language and then, when in that foreign country, are incapable of communication. There are shades of knowledge, but let's be clear that memorized should mean memorized.
>
> This is hard work, and this book is working with the assumption that its readers will be learning pieces from scratch. In this context, "learning" includes memorization.

Landmarks

You now have your practice log, and now it is time to get organized. The practice log does more than remind you of which pieces you have practiced and which you need to do. It also helps you keep track of landmarks.

Landmarks are, in short, rehearsal letters. (Orchestral players know what these are, but keyboardists may not. These are editorial letters in scores so that the conductor can tell everyone to start at "C" or "D" or wherever. This works beautifully, except when the conductor has a different edition from the rest of the orchestra.)

As you know, solo repertoire doesn't come with rehearsal letters, so you are going to have to make your own. Before getting into how to do that, we should consider why we're doing this.

Landmarks are those places to which you will jump backward or forward when you have a memory slip. (I write "when" because it is going to happen sooner or later.) Landmarks need to be in logical places, and they also have to be in locations where you will be able to make a seamless transition. In other words, landmarks should be where phrases naturally rest. Yes, it is really important to know the music theory behind your score, but you don't necessarily need to know the theory to find the phrases. Use your ear and your instinct.

Placing landmarks is kind of fun, because it is nice to see a piece break up into manageable sections. Sometimes in a piece with which I am familiar, I am able to mark landmarks right away. If I don't know a piece too well, I will add landmarks much more cautiously, only marking them out as I work my way through the memorization.

Sometimes I use actual letters, but the problem with letters is this: they are much too firm. For instance, when I was working on the third movement of Bach's D-Minor Harpsichord Concerto, I finally got around to working on my letter "N," only to find that my "N" was much too long. Since I had already written "O," the temptation was to just deal with the long "N" and tolerate the fact that the landmark was too big. That is not good practice, however. (Remember *patience*?) So, I ended up creating N1 and N2, a simple solution.

In order to avoid the lettering problem, I tend to draw asterisks in my scores, and those little stars serve as landmarks. I don't always feel a need to enumerate landmarks; I only need to know they are there.

Some authors on memorization have written that you should be able to play from anywhere in a piece. They also suggest jumping around in your practice, apparently so that you will be able to recover from anywhere in the score. This only confuses matters. Knowing that audiences expect musical phrases, we can assume that musically placed landmarks will help you survive memory slips in the most musical manner. Jumping from, say, measure 101 to measure 55 just because you *can* is not a musical decision. Be logical, be musical.

Once those landmarks are placed, begin work on the piece. (Don't forget: they can always be changed or moved.) Often I do the following: I memorize the final landmark and then go to the first, then to the penultimate, then to the second. This seems to pace things patiently, and it keeps me from becoming too excited about finishing a piece. I have memorized pieces where the last page isn't memorized as well as the rest of the piece. That happens when I have rushed the process out of impatient excitement. (Well, it *is* fun to finish a lengthy project!)

If I am learning a long piece, I sometimes leapfrog my landmarks (A-C-E-G, etc.). After that, I fill in the blanks (ABC, CDE, EFG, and so on). If I am working on a piece in which I might not be exactly sure where I will ultimately put landmarks, I might begin at the top of each page and work my way down till I find a suitable phrase ending. All in all, seek variety in your practice, while also making choices that serve the memorization process itself.

This brings me to the most important part of landmark work. *Once a piece is memorized, one must know the landmarks backwards and forwards.* Indeed, knowing the landmarks becomes, in some ways, more important than knowing individual notes. Make sure you are able to start from each landmark; that you know where each landmark sits in the score; and that you are able to visualize each landmark's starting point. When I have a piece memorized and am working away from the instrument, I don't visualize the piece from beginning to end. Instead, I work from the last landmark to the first, making sure I am fully able to jump to any section of the piece at any time.

Finally, a word with regard to concertos: In a concerto, you have nowhere to go but forward. The orchestra is dragging you along, but only in the forward direction. (Or perhaps you are dragging the orchestra along!) In a solo piece, however, you can easily get caught in a loop or start over again. Thus I tend to think of concertos as two-dimensional. They can only go in a temporal line from here to there. Solo repertoire is three-dimensional. With a memory slip, solo repertoire has the potential to go up, down, left, right, backwards, forwards. Thank God for landmarks!

You Say Memory, I Say Mnemonic

Once after a recital, an audience member approached me with the usual memorization question: "How do you do it?"

My response was, "Well, it's not really memorization. I use a bunch of mnemonics to create the experience—but if I didn't have those tools, the piece wouldn't be memorized."

"But you just played a recital from memory!" he replied.

Silly me, he was right. I was, in fact, playing from memory, but my perception was from the business end. I was doing *hard work* while this audience member was experiencing something that appeared effortless.

Look at the Wikipedia entry on *mnemonic*:

> A **mnemonic**, or **mnemonic device**, is any learning technique that aids information retention. Mnemonics aim to translate information into a form that the human brain can retain better than its original form. Even the process of merely learning this conversion might already aid in the transfer of information to long-term memory. Commonly encountered mnemonics are often used for lists and in auditory form, such as short poems, acronyms, or memorable phrases, but mnemonics can also be used for other types of information and in visual or kinesthetic forms. Their use is based on the observation that the human mind more easily remembers spatial, personal, surprising, physical, sexual, humorous, or otherwise 'relatable' information, rather than more abstract or impersonal forms of information.
>
> The word *mnemonic* is derived from the ancient Greek word μνημονικός (*mnēmonikos*), meaning 'of memory' and is related to Mnemosyne ('remembrance'), the name of the goddess of memory in Greek mythology. Both of these words are derived from μνήμη (*mnēmē*), 'remembrance, memory.' Mnemonics in antiquity were most often considered in the context of what is today known as the art of memory.
>
> Ancient Greeks and Romans distinguished between two types of memory: the 'natural' memory and the 'artificial' memory. The former is inborn, and is the one that everyone uses automatically and without thinking. The artificial memory in contrast has to be trained and developed through the learning and practicing of a variety of mnemonic techniques.

> Mnemonic systems are special techniques or strategies consciously used to improve memory, it helps employ information already stored in long-term memory to make memorization an easier task. (accessed February 19, 2014)

Is there ever a case in musical memorization when one *isn't* using mnemonics? Sure, some ingrained tunes require no memory device (for example, *Twinkle, Twinkle, Little Star*), but, for the purpose of memorizing music to play in concert, a large majority of the work is based in mnemonic memory.

Remember the three types of memory: tactile, aural, and visual. Because mnemonics play such an important role in memorizing music, it almost seems as if they should be considered a fourth type of memory. But mnemonics are tools, not actual memory.

I use mnemonics to create all three types of memory. From landmarks to form, from harmony to visualization of chord shapes, mnemonics guide the memorization process from the inception to the final stages.

All in all, more people have done much deeper research into memory than I have, and I don't want to get into a debate about exactly what types of memory might exist. For the memorizing musician, it is important to consider which type, when, and how memory is being used. For me, the simplification of memory types has been helpful, and I like to keep three: tactile, visual, and aural. You may want to consider more possibilities. After all, it is your brain and your performance.

A Discernible Regularity

While it is clear that not everyone agrees on memory types, I will admit that I am not always sure when a mnemonic is memory and when memory is a mnemonic. I am not a strong advocate for memorizing music already in one's fingers, and, as a general rule, I *never* listen to recordings in order to get to know the music I am working on.

That said, let's presume that, in the early stages of memorization, just about everything is a mnemonic. The big advantage to this approach is that you won't develop tactile memory early on. This advantage will play out later when you might experience self-doubt during a performance: you'll have your mnemonics to rely upon.

Landmarks are mnemonics on a grand scale. I make them a part of my daily routine and find that they are essential to a successfully memorized performance. Because landmarks don't come right away, you should begin by memorizing just a few measures a day.

Repetition plays an extremely significant role in the memorization of even the simplest passage. You might find yourself repeating the same measures over and over again. The goal should not be to create a tactile memory experience, however. Repetition can be used to create aural memory, but aural memory is difficult to maintain when a piece is being learned from scratch.

My repetitious practice creates a comprehension of pattern. I like the Wikipedia definition of pattern: "a discernible regularity in the world or in a manmade design" (accessed February 19, 2014). In musical terms, that pattern could be a simple regularity of notes, and it could also be the regularity of harmony or rhythm. It can be any combination of those three and possibly even other elements.

Presuming that you have already created a phrase-influenced landmark in a piece, repetition of that phrase should help you discern its patterns. Be careful: don't let your repetition engrain tactile memory. Here a timer and metronome become important. Limit your time of repetitious practice while also keeping your metronome tempo slow so as to avoid tactile memory.

Obviously, the memorization of an entire piece will be made up of many different types of memorization techniques, from small-scale patterns to large forms. In the end, the performer may not even remember the process that led to full memorization, especially if this slow process results in excellent aural and visual memory. Regardless of how one ultimately retains a piece, small-scale patterns create essential mnemonics for the early stages of memorization.

But Wait … There's More!

Repetitious practice is not always the best practice, but it can't be ignored. In my worst, most impatient type of practice, I tended to repeat and repeat. I was just too anxious to get the piece to playing level, and all I wanted to do was *play*.

This sort of practice can be thoughtless. Even if it isn't thoughtless, it does little else but to assure a tactile foundation. Those musicians who bring a piece to playing level before attempting to memorize it have probably not done much more than repeat passages after, perhaps, marking fingerings and other foundational notes. After a point, it may be possible to play such work from memory, but is this really as far as you want to prepare before going on stage?

What are some other early memorization techniques? There is no one way to do this; you must always be creative with your approach.

For keyboardists, consistent fingering is essential, and the same can be said for string players. Fingering is ultimately a tactile practice, and, as with all tactile memorization, it shouldn't be your only means of retention. There have been times when I have lost my fingering while on stage and have had to rely on my aural and/or visual memory to get myself back on track.

What about form? Let's look at the slow movement of Bach's D-Minor Harpsichord Concerto. I began work on this by putting in landmarks, and that process inevitably raised the question of the movement's form. This is a simple form, essentially a series of episodes flanked by a *ritornello*. Knowing that the *ritornello* only occurs at the beginning and at the end of the movement has helped me understand where to put some landmarks while also minimizing my work. (That is, if I learn the first *ritornello*, I don't need to learn the final one since they are identical.) Looking closer at the form, I see that the *ritornello* functions like an *ostinato* bass, occurring regularly throughout the entire movement.

> In case you thought that music theory class was boring, you might be realizing that understanding harmony and form is important to memorization. From a simple refrain form (like a *ritornello* with an *ostinato bass*) to bigger concepts like sonata form, it is important to know how your music is constructed. A little harmonic analysis helps a lot in the learning process, so don't be afraid to use one of your practice sessions to map out exactly how your piece is put together.

What about harmony? With that same concerto movement and now recognizing the ostinato bass, you can use harmony to help your memorization. For instance, the opening *ritornello* is in G minor. When repeated as a bass line with melody (my "A" landmark), we are in G minor, closing to a C minor cadence. In the next section (my "B" landmark), we start in C minor, but the ostinato bass appears a few bars later in D minor, eventually cadencing in B-flat major. Some sequences and other harmonic machinations occur, all eventually bringing us back to G minor.

None of this formal and harmonic analysis is worth publishing in a scholarly journal. I did this in sketch form for my own purpose: to memorize. With that in mind, you don't have to come up with a hardcore analysis. Simply do what works for you, but make sure that whatever you are doing is going to bring you to a better level of memorization. Think of these small steps as mnemonics towards the greater goal of memorized music.

Sometimes I work and work on a piece, and parts of it simply won't stick. One way of dealing with this is to take time off, something I will discuss in a later chapter. By getting away from the piece for a few days or an even longer period of time, I might return and find the piece in a better place than when I left it. It is hard to judge whether and how such mental rest will work, so you might not want to count on it. A more reliable technique would be to play through your piece as you might have already been doing. Every time you get stuck, write down the location, taking detailed notes of the problem spots. In reality, you might find fewer sticky places than you originally thought. This process in itself leads to better memorization, and it also gives you a practical foundation from which you can fix any problems.

I am not always this intellectual in my memorization practice. In the case of one difficult contemporary piece, I used the fingering to help me memorize the right hand. It was tactile work though mnemonic in its own right, but it was with the goal of creating aural memory. The visual memory will follow once I have a better sense of how the piece "goes."

Developing Aural Memory

Nothing helps advance memorization practice like actually knowing how a piece sounds. From that point, having a good ear and being able to apply that ear to your instrument will make the memorization process move quickly.

There are various degrees of knowing how a piece sounds, of course. You may have heard something for many years, giving you the freedom to play the piece by ear. Or perhaps you have heard a piece several times, and you can pick out many, but not all, of the notes without a score.

What if you have never heard the work before? Many musicians will turn to recordings to help get to know a piece. This is a bad idea. You will learn another performer's interpretation, and that interpretation will stick in your ear when you start playing the piece. Maybe you will try to solve this problem by listening to several different interpretations. Nevertheless, you simply can't know what effect this is going to have on your own interpretation. In order to be authentic to yourself, you should make your own interpretive decisions. Skip the recordings and allow yourself to learn a piece the right way: the slow way. Patience!

If you are working on a contemporary work, recordings might not even be available. In many cases, you have a unique advantage: you can talk to the composer. Many composers won't tell you how to play their music (although *some* will insist), but they can give you an idea of what it is they had in mind when writing the piece.

(Here is a thought for those who disagree with my stance on not listening to recordings: What were the composers listening to when writing your piece? They didn't need a recording to figure out how it sounds.)

One of the hardest things to memorize is a piece you thought you heard differently. With something already in your ear, it is hard to erase it. That in mind, you should be careful about what and whom you listen to.

In conservatory I had a colleague who had a brilliant memory. He had no money to buy scores, so he would take them out of the library on Friday night, memorize them over the weekend, and then return them to the library on Monday. When it got time for performance class, the other students would enjoy following his playing with the score, because he had surely memorized incorrect notes and wrong dynamics. He did have a brilliant memory, but he was sloppy in its application.

There is one genre for which I advocate recordings: concertos. Recordings can be used to learn your cues. Since rehearsal time with orchestra is always limited, knowing your cues cold is extremely helpful, and, while you could use your imagination, nothing helps like knowing more or less how the orchestration should sound.

If you have never heard your piece before, your aural memory might come last in the process. You can be assured that, if it is last, you have got a solid foundation to work with. Just be patient, and let your three memory types work slowly together to create well-rounded retention.

And what about developing a better ear? That is an entirely different topic. Suffice it to say that you can never have too good an ear.

Working Away from the Instrument

Until this point I have written a lot about working at the instrument. (I should point out that, by "instrument," I also mean the *voice*. A singer's instrument is just that: an instrument.) What about working away from the instrument?

On the whole, I strive to spend as much time working away from the instrument as I spend working at the instrument. Because there are many stages to the memorization process, a 50/50 ratio doesn't always work out. Here is my own secret: I don't really *enjoy* working away from the instrument. That doesn't mean that I *shouldn't*, so I must force myself to make it a part of my daily practice.

I suspect many musicians don't enjoy working away from the instrument. I, for one, simply enjoy playing too much. Sitting on a sofa and visualizing my score isn't lots of fun. Nevertheless, working away from the instrument remains probably the best way to develop quickly a visual and even aural memory.

Visual memory isn't just about "seeing" the score. Some visual memory can be related to how one imagines chord shapes or hand positions at the instrument. It can also be how one envisions a musical form. All in all, the best visual skills come from working away from the instrument. In fact, what we are really talking about here is mental practice, as opposed to physical practice.

Many times in my day-to-day routine, I don't feel like practicing a specific piece or practicing at all. Keeping my practice agenda concise and creative helps me stay motivated and inspired. In that same vein, I keep my mental practice as varied as possible. Not only does this help to keep me interested, it also prevents the work from becoming routine and, therefore, thoughtless.

Here are some techniques:
- Do mental practice away from the instrument. Use a different room, use a different chair. Go outside, even if for a ten-minute session. Use your mental practice as an opportunity to stand up and not be sedentary. Whoever said that cerebral work didn't burn calories?
- Apply everything already discussed to your mental practice: landmarks, metronome, mnemonics.
    - Landmarks: Jump around. If you know all your landmarks, don't visualize your piece in forward order. Go from Z to A. Or skip every other landmark. Make sure you can visualize the start of each landmark.

- o   Metronome: Use a metronome for mental practice. It will keep you from mentally rushing the easy spots.
- o   Mnemonics: Visualize those patterns and differences in patterns. This is really helpful when in the early learning stages. When you return to the instrument, you will identify those patterns much quicker.
- Visualize a piece straight through. Although hard to do early in the memorization process, it does help develop aural memory. Later on, once a piece is more or less memorized, a straight-through visualization can become a valuable exercise in concentration.
- Can't sleep at night? Try some mental practice. If it doesn't help you sleep, at least you are doing something with the wasted time. You can also do mental practice while out for solitary walks or sitting in a park.

What about learning a score completely away from the instrument? Why not? Many musicians practice this. Give it a try if you have never done it before. Take a new, short piece and spend a couple of weeks on it *away* from the instrument. When you finally bring it to the instrument, you might surprise yourself with how well you have learned it.

Those Slow Pieces

When I first returned to playing from memory, I started researching memorization techniques on the internet. If you have done a similar search, you know there is quite a bit of information available. Back then I came upon a site that briefly discussed how to work on slow pieces. The general suggestion was to play them quickly. The logic, as I understood, was to establish tactile memory as a foundation and then eventually slow the piece down to the desired tempo.

You already know my view on establishing a foundation of tactile memory. Let's explore what else is wrong with that approach, not only because it applies to slow pieces. It applies to all repertoire.

> It *is* true that learning a slow movement by playing it fast can work. I have done it, although I no longer do so. What is it we are trying to achieve, however?
>
> By learning and playing slow pieces quickly, we are affecting the manner in which we will ultimately perform them. Just as listening to recordings will influence our personal interpretations, this method will inhibit our ultimate goal of transcendent performance. In short, it is *unmusical*.
>
> Aside from this highfalutin talk, there is the practical issue of the very nature of slow music: Slow music is *slow*, making it easy to lose one's concentration and get lost in the lack of activity. Therefore, slow music requires the highest level of visual and aural memory. Building a solely tactile foundation in order to achieve this will ultimately fail.
>
> To practice memorizing slow movements, the metronome should be set at least twenty-five percent slower than the optimal tempo. This is recommended not only for mental work, but also for work at the instrument. The metronome will keep you from speeding through the long, slow notes, both mentally and physically.
>
> I do the same for my faster movements. Indeed, I apply this approach to my entire repertoire, regardless of final tempo.

Daily Routine, with Variety

I begin my practice routine by writing down my goals for the day. This gives me a sense of what I am going to do, of course, but it also helps me come up with a realistic time frame, and it keeps me from practicing with little regard for my own endurance. Breaks need to be scheduled.

My daily goals include numeric indications:
- a ratio-like marking, such as 15:10, indicating for me that I'll do 15 minutes of mental work and 10 at the instrument
- metronome markings, usually a slower one for mental work and a slightly faster one for instrument work.

By creating daily goals, I can work toward variety in my practice. It is so easy to get stuck in a routine, and routines result in unproductive practice. I often find inspiration for variety by looking at my notes from the previous practice session. I cannot stress enough the need to maintain thoughtful, varied practice. Establishing your daily goals is an excellent way to accomplish this.

I like to use a table and chair for mental practice. Formerly I used the sofa, but my poor posture created poor results. My practice space also includes a music stand. The stand sits next to the instrument, and I put my score on the stand when a piece is becoming really solid. This assures that my eyes aren't on any music, but it allows me to easily refer to the score if I get into trouble.

At the earliest stages of memory, I am either working completely away from the instrument or dividing my time between mental and instrument work. I work by landmarks, and I tend to jump around a lot with my landmarks. This is part of my drive for variety in practice. Moreover, if I were always to start from the beginning, I wouldn't be developing a fully dimensional understanding of the piece.

One of the great challenges in the early stages of memorization is time. When starting a piece, not a lot of time is required. You are working mentally, possibly at the instrument, but you can only do so much. Once the piece gets closer to total memorization, however, you need more time to think through and play through all of the landmarks. Fortunately, once a piece is totally memorized, the time window contracts, and you will need less time. This reality may make you want to stagger your work so that everything isn't reaching maximum practice time at the same time.

Knowing When to Take Time Off

Back in my conservatory days, my piano teacher Michael Ruiz was firm in his belief that one should practice every piece during every practice day. This is an approach that I still cling to, and, for each of my practice sessions, I make an effort to touch each piece I am working on, even if only for a few minutes. By using my daily goals, I can map out whatever I hope to achieve that day. One advantage of this approach, of course, is that everything remains at the forefront at all times.

This approach might seem like a disadvantage. Because I work on everything every day, I am limited to how much I can handle each day. Wouldn't it be nice to be working on more music? This approach, however, assures a kind of self-censorship, and it keeps me from biting off more than I can chew.

I don't recall my piano teacher discussing when to take time off. Time off is a really healthy thing, since we musicians can become unhealthily obsessed with our work. When I entered Yale, I was used to practicing nearly six hours a day. When it came time to dole out the practice room schedule, my harpsichord teacher Richard Rephann said three hours per day would probably be enough. I was shocked! Maybe Richard was telling me something about quality over quantity. At that time, three hours a day felt like nothing, and graduate school started to feel like a permanent vacation.

Since then I have come to respect the need for a day or even days without practice. Sometimes I schedule two intense practice days and then take a day off. If I aim for three intense days, I find that I am beat by the third day, and I don't practice as well afterwards. If I am in that sort of situation, I might use the third day to play through my music more for enjoyment than for intensive study.

To the pianist Arthur Rubinstein is attributed the comment that if he missed a day of practice, he noticed; if he missed two days, the critics noticed; and if he missed three days, the audience noticed. When I am preparing a recital, I turn to Rubinstein's wisdom. I never like to take time off when a recital is just a few days away.

When working in the early stages of memorization, however, I don't feel that one needs to be so dogmatic. In fact, time away from the instrument helps music grow internally. It also helps to rekindle the passion for the repertoire.

> I am writing this chapter on a day off. Yesterday my work on the third movement of Bach's D-Minor Concerto went very well—so well, in fact, that I imagined it would be ready to go within a week or so. Last night I woke up around 1 a.m., and, as a means to help me fall back to sleep, I started working my way through the movement mentally. Before I fell asleep again, I got hung up somewhere around my "L" landmark, and I realized that the piece still needs more mental work with the score before I can run the entire movement in my mind.
>
> When I return to practice tomorrow, you can be assured that I will be strongly motivated to fix that L landmark. My day off was planned before my sleepless memory slip, but having a day off is helping me to process any impatience I have in learning the Bach. Being away from the instrument today is making me excited about tomorrow's practice session. Indeed, I am even getting excited as I write about it! The Bach is *close*, but forcing the issue by working in a dogmatic, non-stop way is not going to get me where I need to be. A day off is a nice tonic.

Taking an Old Friend to Heart

New repertoire needs to be memorized as it is learned, as opposed to learned and then memorized. I have also asserted that, if a piece is not memorized, it is not learned.

As you know, I firmly believe that tactile memory is the weakest form of memory. This is why scratch learning is so important, as it keeps tactile memory from taking precedence over intellectual (that is, visual and aural) memory. If, however, you already have a piece in your repertoire but not memorized, how are you going to memorize it?

Begin by approaching the piece as if you don't already know it. After placing your landmarks, spend some days doing only mental practice with a metronome. You might surprise yourself by how much you know; you might also be discouraged by how little you know. In your mental work, reinforce your landmarks. Be able to see them and hear them cold.

After a few days, set up a daily schedule beginning with mental work and followed by work at the instrument. At the instrument, work only from your landmarks, slowly with a metronome, and resist the temptation to play through the piece. Are you able to visualize and play the first few notes of each landmark?

You might need some remedial memory work. Use the techniques described previously in this book. Find patterns in the music. Use analytical techniques to bring you to a greater understanding of the piece. The good news is that you probably already have a strong aural sense of the piece, so don't be afraid to use your ear as much as possible.

When you finally come around to some fairly thorough memorization, play the piece slowly with the metronome, but make sure that you are thinking of each landmark before you play it. Congratulations! You've now reached the middle stage of memorization. I will discuss this stage in the next section of this book, along with techniques for making your piece ready for performance.

Above all, assume nothing, and make sure that you have approached your old friend with as much care and attention as you have been giving your new friends.

Now You're Dancing on Air!

Do you always find that the *learning* of the music is more fun than the *performing* of the music? I do. There is a certain feeling when all of your landmarks are learned, you are able to play them straight through, and you finally get the piece to click. You're dancing on air! What a wonderful, affirming feeling. All of your hard work comes together in one transcendent moment.

But—sigh—now you have got to keep things afloat. This brings us to the next section of this book: The Middle Stage of Memorization. Much needs to be done in order to keep your piece dancing on air, fresh and ready for performance. This is where work becomes *work*. You see, the memorization part of this journey is just the beginning. Now you have to learn how to maintain the memory without becoming an automaton in performance. You also have to learn how to deal with nerves and fear. You haven't danced on air for an audience yet.

Touching the Void

The 2003 documentary film, *Touching the Void*, details a near-fatal attempt to climb Siula Grande in the Peruvian Andes. At one point in the film, one of the climbers comments that going up is hard, but descending is much more difficult and dangerous. In spite of the relief of successfully climbing the mountain, the descent requires much more attention.

Memorization is just like that. It is difficult to bring a piece to memory, but much harder to maintain it and perform it after the arduous learning process. The descent requires much more attention.

If you have followed all of the suggestions set forth here, then you have developed some good habits around your repertoire. I assure you that what we have covered is more than half the battle. With your good habits having set a firm foundation, this next stage will be even more challenging. It might even be tedious, because it is not really learning. It is maintenance and planning.

How are you going to minimize your practice so that your performance is inspired? At the same time, how are you going to maximize your practice so that, when on stage, you don't have a single doubt about your mastery of memorization? This is hard work. It takes planning and patience.

Whew! Be prepared to find out if you truly love what you do.

THE MIDDLE STAGE OF MEMORIZATION

You've Got It! ... (or so You Think)

Now you have a good foundation with your piece. In fact, you are able to play it through completely by heart with only a little bump here or there. Maybe you have even played it *perfectly* once or twice.

Now what are you going to do? You feel pretty good about it, but you are nervous about playing it in public. On a good day, you can play the piece really well, but on a bad day you don't feel completely ready.

Welcome, friend, to the Middle Stage of Memorization, a musical purgatory that lies between the early excitement of memorizing a piece and the late confidence of knowing that you have a solid piece in your repertoire.

Here is the problem: The early stages of memorization have clear goals. You need to get from A to Z, and, as I have been outlining, there are clear ways to do that. At this point, it is hard to assess your goals when you are so close to performance-level memory. Am I ready yet? Do I need to do more? How will I know when I am ready? Scheduling a performance in order to find out the answers is not a wise strategy.

The middle stage creates its own impatience. You are almost there, but not yet. How much mental practice do you need to do? Should you just play through the piece until it's perfect? When should you add new repertoire to memorize? Will this process ever be over?

Most important, *when can you let a piece rest?* You have spent so much time bringing your piece to this level, but how do you know when enough is enough?

These are all challenging questions to answer, and you may find yourself quite unsettled at this point. This section of the book will address the issues and present some techniques and methods for finding answers.

Respect!

In "Daily Routine, with Variety" I discussed the need to keep variety in one's daily practice. It is far too simple to do the same thing day after day. Now that you have a foundation and have entered this middle stage, it is time to reassess your daily routine. (Of course, I advocate this reassessment on a daily basis, but this middle stage will require a higher level of assessment. You are in a new place now.)

With your solid foundation, you will find that you don't have to do the same thing every day. There is nothing wrong with just playing your pieces, and you should not feel obligated to do mental work and landmark work every day. At the same time, you don't want to let your foundation slide, so you might want to alternate days of mental/landmark work with "performance" days. Whatever you do, let your planning and decision making be conscious, and avoid letting routine become a crutch.

You have only so much time in your practice day, so it is still important to keep working with a timer and a practice log, especially when you have to maintain your discipline with other pieces you are working on. It is terribly easy to get excited when you are *finally* able to play an entire piece after having spent so much time crawling through those early stages of memory. With that in mind, you need to remember that this middle stage is still only a stage in the learning process.

I write these thoughts from experience. You will remember that I had some significant memory slips when I returned to memorization practice after so many years. Missing from my work was a respect for this middle stage. I had quickly memorized my pieces (the early stage, but much too fast) and then naively paraded them out in performance without respecting the need to develop a firm post-memorized foundation.

After spending so much time memorizing your piece, the unfortunate fact is that you are just not there yet. If you embrace this stage as a learning stage, however, you will approach the concert stage with the confidence of knowing that you can, indeed, play by heart. Hang in there. Respect the process.

Mental Techniques

Now that you made it through the early stages of memorization, you already have some good mental practice techniques. You also know that mental practice is essential to successfully playing by heart. With your regular mental practice, you will maintain and improve your visual, aural, and, to some extent, tactile memories.

The difficulty at this stage is to sustain freshness and alertness while doing what is necessary to keep a piece internalized. In order to be fresh and alert, you need to maintain some variety in your practice. Otherwise you might find yourself in thoughtless routine, and that could lead to some unfortunate surprises when you bring your piece out in public. Because I am least motivated when it comes to mental practice, I find that this is the area where I have to be the most conscientious about finding variety in my practice.

You already read about some mental practice techniques. Practice with landmarks, such as leapfrogging landmarks, visualizing A then C then E, eventually returning to B then D then F, and so on. Work backwards, starting at the end and then working, in reverse order, through each landmark. Try to do this work with metronome, sometimes well below tempo and other times at or near optimal tempo. (Oddly, my optimal mental tempo is usually a few notches slower than my optimal performance tempo. I am not quite sure why, but it could be that I am more careful—that is, less tactile—when working a piece mentally.)

If you are short on time or you really feel confident about a piece, you can just review the starting points of each landmark. From there, go on to play the piece directly. Generally speaking, mental work at this stage takes less time than the playing work, but that doesn't mean it is any less important.

As you become more and more confident in your mental work and the playing of the piece, you can alternate days of mental work and days of playing work. This is not so much about time constraints as about keeping things fresh and varied. By taking a day off from playing in favor of a day of mental work, new interpretive insights emerge from the silence.

There is an endless variety of ways to diversify your mental practice. The most important thing is to keep it varied and to make sure that your choices are conscious. For those reasons, continue to work with a practice log, a timer, daily goals, a metronome ... all of those good habits. This isn't to say, however, that you can't enjoy the occasional unplanned mental practice session on the beach, in moments of insomnia, or in walking meditation.

Playing Techniques

In the same day's practice session, mental work should precede playing work. In real life that happens. You would never do mental work *after* playing a recital, for instance—unless you are reliving the recital, good or bad, in a post-concert restless night!

Once again, alternate days of mental work with days of playing work. With less time in your practice session, you might just touch on, for instance, your landmarks. Envision each landmark's starting point, and play the start of each landmark instead of the entire piece. For me, this works best in reverse order.

Let's presume that you have become sure of your piece and found a comfortable, though varied, practice routine of mental and playing work. You are quite confident in your memorization and in your interpretation of the piece, but you want to make sure that your piece is truly ready to go. Other than jumping around from landmark to landmark, by which other ways can you vary your playing work?

First, you could simply play through the entire piece for fun. By "for fun," I mean that you are playing in a manner that is completely relaxed without much attention to landmarks or visual memory. For me, it is rare when this type of playing happens in concert. If it does happen, it is usually followed by a memory slip when I start to realize that I am playing before a live audience. This "for fun" playing shouldn't become a regular thing, but it is nice to remind yourself how fun it is to actually play well without any stress. When on stage, we need to give the appearance of this relaxation, but we have to be extremely conscious of what we are doing. All told, I wouldn't recommend this type of playing more than twice a week. It can be harmful to what you are trying to achieve.

Second, in contrast to the "for fun" playing, try super-concentrated playing. Force yourself to anticipate each landmark, to visualize it before you get there. Try to visualize every note while playing, especially in fast music, thus overriding any tactile response. You don't want this type of self-consciousness to happen in concert, but, if it does when, say, you are excessively nervous, you will be ready to handle it. Another reason to force landmark anticipation and visualization is to keep your mind where it needs to be: on the music. It is all too easy in this middle stage of memorization to play "for fun" with little regard for focus and detail.

Try to make yourself nervous by deliberately creating memory slips. In doing so, you can practice working your way out of a slip, either by jumping to an earlier or to a later landmark. In some cases, you won't be in a spot where it is easy to jump to a landmark, so you must force yourself to improvise until you find yourself in a place for smooth and convenient transition. (New to improvisation? Hang in there: I will touch on it later.) Importantly, *don't do too much of this type of practice.* Nervousness can be a learned response, and you might find yourself establishing some specific and regular memory slip areas.

My harpsichord teacher John Whitelaw talked about a *Doppelgänger* technique in which the performer while playing would picture him- or herself as an audience member. Although John and I were working with music from score, this technique has excellent applications to the memorizing musician. It takes a little practice, but you will find that you will hear the music differently—indeed, like an audience member. This in itself can add a bit of nervousness and realism to the play-through experience.

> A *Doppelgänger* is a fictional concept of a paranormal double. In the folklore, one sees oneself, and this experience is usually the harbinger of bad luck. Abraham Lincoln is said to have seen his own *Doppelgänger* shortly before being elected to his second term—a term he never completed, of course. (Wikipedia, accessed March 10, 2014)
>
> But that's just folklore. Your own *Doppelgänger* is going to help you to become an excellent performer!

A similar technique is to record yourself and treat the recording as though it needs to be perfect. I am generally not in favor of this process because one ends up modifying the interpretation more and more to fit the particular circumstances of the recording instead of working purely with one's ear. It is a bit like looking at oneself in a funhouse mirror, with the resulting image a distortion of reality.

With all of this playing and the excitement about finally being able to play through a piece after so much work, we cannot forget one of the most important playing techniques: to not play at all and to work mentally through the score. Don't neglect your mental work.

Trap Doors

Another playing technique during the middle stage of memorization is to identify and work with "trap doors," passages that look, sound, and/or feel similar to other areas in the same piece. These can be in the same key, but you might even find trap doors in different keys. When one is unaware of a trap door, it is easy to jump from that place to an entirely different location. This would not be so bad if you didn't jump too far, but, in one case, I found myself in a trap door that opened at the beginning of a piece and took me to about twenty measures from the end. (The audience should have gotten its money back.)

An obvious example of a trap door would be jumping from the exposition directly to the recapitulation in a sonata form movement. In a simple binary form, it might be easy to mistake a B-section coda for something that should occur early on in the A-section. Some trap doors may not even be related to the form of the piece and, instead, to where various pitches or phrases lie. A solitary F#, for instance, might just trigger a movement to the wrong place.

> Once again, understanding some basic form and analysis is important to the memorization process. If you know about sonata form and its exposition-development-recapitulation progression, you can easily identify where the same musical ideas will be presented in different keys and, in most cases, exactly what those keys should be.

At this stage in your practice, you need to identify every single trap door. Even if you are playing your pieces straight through without any problems, it is important to realize that memory slips can occur, and you must prepare for them before they occur. To that end, knowing the location of each trap door is as important as knowing your landmarks. Make sure that, if you fall through a trap door, you have an exit strategy that doesn't include ending your piece several minutes early.

I often unwittingly uncover trap doors right before a recital performance. I owe this to self-consciousness rather than my usually relaxed practice. In fact, I have uncovered trap doors during my warm-up time just before a concert, which is extremely nerve wracking. Because this has happened several times, I make every effort possible to find those nasty places early in the memorization process. Not always so evident, you may not identify them until you have memorized the piece and entered the middle stage of memorization.

Previously I wrote about the practice technique of making yourself nervous. You can use your trap doors to create memory slip-like situations. Once you have created such a situation, try to come up with as many escape routes as possible, including improvisation. You can't guarantee that exactly the same scenario will occur in concert, but a familiarity with all of your options will help you to handle any crisis with grace and *élan*.

Are We There Yet?

You think you have done all you can, but you keep asking the question, "Is it ready yet?"

How much time have you actually put into your piece? How much *more* time do you need to put into your piece? (You can see why repertoire selection is so important: you have devoted so much time to this process that you probably don't want to play anything but A-list music.)

Some pianists I know will boldly claim that it takes them a week or two to memorize a piece. Pay no attention to these music jocks. You know by now that it is not about speed, but about patience. The fact is that your piece is never entirely ready. You can always do more with it, not only interpretively, but also in the manner in which you hold it in your heart.

What you are really trying to find out is whether an empirical way exists to determine a memorized piece is "ready to go." Some musicians avoid the question almost entirely by putting a piece to sleep for a certain length of time before bringing it out again and preparing it for performance. I feel that this is a valuable approach, although it only changes the question from "When is it ready to perform?" to "When is it ready to be put to sleep?"

As we are about to leave the middle stage of memorization, there is one last step I take before feeling truly ready for a recital: practice performances.

Practice Performances

If you have just one or two pieces, you should begin by playing them for a close friend. That friend must make you nervous, so be careful about whom you ask. Chances are that you won't be happy with that one performance, so think about playing the same pieces for that same friend a week later. Whatever you do, try to replicate the performance experience as much as possible. Be formal, and make sure that your friend is an attentive listener. Value the criticism that the friend gives you, but don't be too hard on yourself.

When you are more confident with your piece or pieces, see if you can schedule them for a relatively low-impact event. Perhaps you could play for friends at a small party, or at a church service, or within the context of a larger chamber music recital. Be careful about some of these choices, however.

Parties may not be the best place, especially if people don't really want to listen or (gasp!) you've been drinking. If you are playing for a church service, especially with a newly memorized piece, make sure it is scheduled as a prelude or early in the service. All of the church service downtime (hymns, readings, sermon, prayers) will build anxiety, and by the time it is your turn to play, you might be in a bad place. Be careful as well about playing a solo piece on a chamber music program. It is sometimes difficult to change from reading-music-mind to playing-from-memory-mind. In short, think hard about where and when you are going to perform.

At times I have used Google+ to create live streams of my practice performances. (Google+ is an online video conferencing service, like Skype. Unlike Skype, though, it is easy to create public video chat rooms.) I have done this for individual works and also for full concerts. With Google+ I don't even need to invite an audience. They just show up when I create a public stream. A few years ago, one of my recitals was cancelled due to snow, so I broadcast the recital via a live stream. A local newspaper picked this up, and I had fifty viewers at one point. You can be assured that the pressures of a live stream are about the same as for a performance in front of an audience. (I only missed having audience feedback, but I did hold up applause signs.)

> PROVIDENCE JOURNAL—ARTS NEWS
>
> **Neither rain, nor snow stops harpsichordist from appointed recital, at least online**
>
> January 21, 2012 11:38 am
> By News staff
>
> Harpsichordist Paul Cienniwa was to perform a program of French baroque music this afternoon at St. Columba's in Middletown. If you had planned to head out to it, be advised, today's snow has changed those plans.
>
> But the show will go on … on the Internet.
>
> Starting at 3 p.m. (the time of the planned St. Columba's concert), Cienniwa will perform the recital live from his home and stream it on the web. You can tune in as early as 2:30 as he tunes up and gets ready.
>
> A program for the recital is also posted on the web.

And now what you've been waiting for. Yes, you can put your piece to rest. Congratulations!

You have now graduated from the Middle Stage of Memorization.

A Few Sticking Points

Fear Factor

Before going on to the final stage of memory, let me address a few items that have gotten swept under the rug. The first one is *fear*.

Without a doubt you will experience memory-related fear at some point in your performing life. As a performer you have already experienced fear and nervousness before going on stage, and you already know not to let that fear take over. You certainly don't want fear to become so much of an issue that you are unable to perform.

Memory-related fear is, for me, a whole different level of performance anxiety. *What if I have a memory slip—will I come to a complete stop? What if I get caught in a loop, and I can't find my way to the end? What if I go completely blank?* At this point, I can't even imagine being nervous for a performance from score. (Here is another reason why working towards memory is such a good thing. It raises the bar so high that everything played with the music seems much easier, and once you get rid of the memory-related fear, everything is even easier.)

Aside from teaching how to memorize, I have been teaching how to create a strong foundation. Think of your landmarks and mnemonics, and think about how you have developed your three memory types so that they work together. You must have confidence in the process, and you must have confidence in your ability to call upon your foundation.

For this reason I advocate practice performances. I already covered them with regard to individual pieces, and I will return to them when I discuss recital preparation. Your practice performances are a part of the confidence-building process. Even if you are already an advanced memorizing performer, you still need to rely on practice performances to work out potential issues that cannot be felt alone in the practice room. One of those issues is fear.

So, dim the lights and prepare for some scary stories as I share some of my own fear anecdotes.

Tales of Fear!

I have a whole bunch of memory slip anecdotes. Those are scary stories in their own right, but this chapter is more about the fear that precedes a performance. Although this book is about memorization, there are no real differences between the fearful feelings preceding a memorized performance and a non-memorized performance.

I think we all know the fear feelings of upset stomachs, restless colons, pounding hearts, clammy palms, sweaty armpits, and shaky hands. To some extent all of this goes away when one becomes a more seasoned performer. As a memorizing musician, you probably have a greater degree of fear than one who doesn't memorize—or, at least in my opinion, your fear is much more justified.

The most fear-inducing occurrence for me is when, just before a performance, I am playing through a piece, and I then have a memory slip. This is quite common! For this reason I always carry my scores with me. I know that I am very well-prepared before a performance, but this is such an irrational event that I, at times, have a hard time visualizing or hearing the correct notes. One solution is to look at the score; another is to start at the previous landmark, after which I have no trouble getting back on track. Ultimately these aren't true slips (even though they *are* slips) in that they are based in a degree of anxiety that, fortunately, doesn't reproduce itself in the focused moments of a performance. My analysis is that, in playing just before a recital, one opens oneself up to a certain amount of nervous distraction, and the results are these irrational memory slips.

I noticed these types of slips early on in my return-to-memory performances, so I got into the habit of a backstage ritual. Because backstage time can build anxiety, I would review all of my landmarks in reverse order, just as I do in my practice. The review had the effect of calming my anxiety and putting me into a good mental state.

However … one time I had a very long wait backstage before a concerto appearance. I had done all of my mental reviewing, and I was pacing a bit backstage. A stagehand came up to me and asked why I had a score in my hand. I said that I was reviewing the music. He, a theater guy, said, "Don't you know the rule about theater?" Of course I didn't: I am a musician. "You never go over your lines before going on stage. That's a sure way to have a mishap."

Since then I try not to review my music just before a performance. If I do any playing on stage before a concert, it is minimal, and I try not to play entire pieces. Backstage I might review my tempi, especially as an accelerated heart rate can make for some hair-raising virtuosity. But now I rest in the confidence of what I knew when I left the house the morning of the performance: I can do this!

The Inner Game

The "Inner Game" is a concept from a book on tennis playing in which author Timothy Gallwey discusses "that which takes place in the mind, played against such elusive opponents as nervousness, self doubt, and fear of failure." Gallwey's approach to tennis playing eventually led to a collaboration with musician Barry Greene and the creation of *The Inner Game of Music* (New York: Doubleday, 1986).

My interpretation of the Inner Game is that it is the little voice running in your head when you are performing. It happens when there is music in front of you, and it happens when you are playing by heart. With music it can be a big distraction; without music it can be deadly. Sometimes a negative voice reminds you how nervous you are. Other times a positive voice tells you things are going really well—after which you invariably make a mistake. The Inner Game will never really go away, so you must learn how to manage it and, if possible, make it work for you. Giving practice performances is an excellent way to find out exactly how your Inner Game is affecting your ability to play from memory. Just like memorization, you need not be afraid of it. You just have to harness it.

In the practice room, the Inner Game is an entirely different problem. Normally you are not nervous in the practice room. The practice room Inner Game here concerns the wandering mind. I am an expert at the wandering mind in the practice room! This is another reason to use a practice log. Should something important come to mind while practicing, jot it down in the log as soon as possible. This has the dual effect of getting it out of one's mind while also helping to remember it later on. The use of landmarks also helps to keep a wandering mind at bay. By working in small sections, you don't have to have a long attention span, and wandering opportunities are minimized.

All in all, it is of utmost importance to recognize the Inner Game when it occurs, both on and off stage. Because what goes on in the practice room invariably influences what happens on stage, it is imperative that you not feed the Inner Game by allowing your mind to wander without any sort of discipline or awareness. And aside from the distracting factor of the Inner Game, you also want to be totally present when playing. After all, that is what you have been working so hard to do.

Total Presence

When I first returned to playing from memory, I became increasingly concerned with the Inner Game. I wasn't so much worried about its role in making me nervous. (After all, I had been playing in public, albeit with music, for a long time, so I was quite used to dealing with the Inner Game.) I was concerned, however, with practice room daydreaming.

In the past, I had already been daydreaming while reading music. The act of memorization, however, made the symptoms of the problem more acute, and I would become angry at myself because I had just played through a piece without much degree of consciousness. If the Inner Game is that overly self-conscious voice that gets in the way of playing, then I was experiencing the complete opposite through daydreamed practice.

I remembered the Buddhist concept of "total presence." This state, often achieved through meditation, puts one in the moment, without distraction or divided attention. Once I realized my problem, I knew that *lack* of total presence was affecting me either with Inner Game-type distraction or non-attention. Either way, I knew I needed to work on this if I was going to practice *and* perform effectively.

> The fact of the matter is that most of us lack total presence in general. Think about how we use smartphones. We are in the middle of a conversation, and we look at our phones. Or think about taking a phone call when you are at the computer. How often are you browsing while on the phone? I am reminded of a couple I observed while on a Caribbean vacation. They were both out for a romantic dinner, but they kept checking their smartphones throughout the meal. Even though I am using technological examples, our lack of total presence reaches back to a time long before microchips. If it didn't, the Buddha would have been out of a job!

I began working on my problem by going through some basic meditation techniques learned over the years. I downloaded a meditation timer app for my phone, and I eventually worked my way up to about fifteen minutes of pre-practice meditation each day. At one point I felt that my meditation skills weren't good enough, so I attended a few meditation sessions at a local Buddhist center.

Not only does meditation have a direct impact on my practice attention, it also gives me something constructive to do backstage. Instead of reviewing my scores or nervously pacing, I am now able to calm myself and focus my mind before going onstage. What a wonderful gift!

I haven't been actively meditating for some time now, but I do call upon my basic meditation skills every time I have a recital to pull together and, especially, backstage. I don't think I will ever be a great meditator, and I don't think I will ever achieve total presence in every aspect of my life. If I can achieve just a fraction of total presence in my performing life, however, then I and, hopefully, my audience will be all the better for it.

A Meditation

Meditation for the purpose of focused, memorized playing doesn't only bring me closer to a state of total presence or provide something to do backstage. Meditation also teaches valuable lessons which, in turn, inform my playing.

First, the act of meditation forces me to be more patient in my work. Patience is challenging, especially when excited about learning new music. You know by now that impatient memorization leads to poor and inconsistent memory. Because the sheer act of calming the mind is such a challenge, meditation gives a new respect to the patient learning process. Meditation, indeed, makes me more patient with myself and with my own limitations.

Second, meditation has a great affect on my ability to handle fear. I think that a lot of the fear we performers experience on stage is about our egos. *I don't want to make a mistake ... I want to appear flawless ... I want to be better than everyone else.* Meditation encourages humility, and in that humility, we are better at accepting our flaws, including those mistakes we make on stage.

Third, meditation helps us appreciate our audiences better. In my initial home meditation, I was simply focusing on calming my mind and trying to develop total presence. When I started to attend group meditation sessions, the focus wasn't on me but on compassion for others. In doing so, I started to think of my audience not as critics, but rather as humans. For me, at least, it is all too easy to become hostile to an audience. *They are too loud ... They aren't listening ... Are they getting it? ... Are they judging me?* Meditation teaches me compassion and a better understanding of humanity.

I truly believe that when we perform, we play ourselves. We open up a window to the universe and expose our souls to our audiences. That is why playing can be so difficult and certainly explains why playing is so personal. If I really do play myself, then isn't it in my best interest as a musician to be as good a person as possible? An audience wouldn't want to see into the soul of a bad person. Like any good, contemplative act, meditation has a way of making us better people. And this informs our playing.

Improvisation

What are your options if you have a memory slip? You could stop playing. You could start all over from the beginning. You could become angry and repeat a passage over and over again, much to the general discomfort of your audience.

These are all terrible ideas. How about this?: You could improvise until you make your way forward or backward to a landmark. Perhaps, however, you don't have any experience with improvisation, especially in front of an audience.

If you do have a slip, it may be possible to jump directly to a landmark. This can work well, depending on the situation. In many cases, you don't have that option, so you need to have a plan. To begin, don't think of improvisation as something you must bring to a high artistic level. Save that for the jazz musicians and the great French cathedral organists. Your improvisation has a practical purpose: to get from A to B—or maybe from B to A. It doesn't need to be anything more than that.

You now know what your improvisation needs to do. Let's consider what it needs to be. First, it needs to stay in the key you are playing in, and it will need to modulate if your next landmark is in another key. If you know your landmarks well, you should know what keys they start in. Second, your improvisation should maintain the rhythm of the phrase and, if necessary, transform itself to the rhythm of where you are headed. Third, your improvisation should maintain the texture of the passage and, again if necessary, develop into the texture of where you intend to arrive.

In other words, your improvisation needs to be in the style of what you are playing. In some ways, that is the easy part, and there is no right or wrong. It merely needs to be persuasive. The more difficult element—modulating to another key—is something you can practice both physically and mentally.

It is possible to practice your improvisation in a pedantic way, working your way through various modulations and making sure that you can get from landmark to landmark. Unfortunately (or fortunately), there isn't that much time in the day to practice in this manner. You can also force memory slips by making yourself nervous, a technique I have discussed.

The bottom line is that the vast majority of your audience (and, most likely, 100% of your audience) won't know that you are improvising. For you, the memory slip moment may feel like an eternity, but you also know, quite rationally, that it is not that big of a moment. This is a game of outwitting the situation, and you have to learn to keep your cool.

This brings us back to fear. Don't forget this: Your audience is not there to hear you make mistakes. They give you the benefit of the doubt in what you are doing, and they will always assume that you are doing the right thing. They are not looking for mistakes, and they really wish you the best so that they can enjoy the performance as much as possible. All you have to do is uphold your end of the bargain by letting them think you have played a perfect performance, whether or not it is true. Keep your cool!

The Memorized Recital

It's Recital Time!

So far, I have taken you from the early stages of memorization, when you were just learning to put a few notes together, to the middle stage of memorization, where you developed a real discipline for maintaining your memorized piece. Now we are fast-forwarding to that point where you have memorized enough repertoire to play a half or full recital. Congratulations!

This is a big leap. You already played some practice performances of your individual pieces, but you now should schedule one or two practice performances of your entire recital. (I hope you have a lot of friends.)

From there, or even before then, you need to book the real deal: not practice performances, but a public recital. Before you book your recital, however, you need to think about how and where those performances are going to take place. The recital venue and format will be important to your success.

Aside from the logistics of venue, you need to think about the logistics of preparing a recital. Sure, you already memorized and practice-performed each piece on the program, but how are you going to keep the ball in the air for an entire recital? If you have let some pieces rest for a while, how are you going to bring them back? This is all a matter of pacing and, to some extent, endurance.

We are almost at the end of this journey, and in the final laps one can become tired, impatient, and sloppy. The weeks before a recital can result in some of the worst, sloppiest practice. We get impatient when we see the finish line, and our minds may already be on other projects.

With careful planning, patience, and deliberate work, you can arrive at your recital knowing that you have made your best effort. Even more important, you will know you are playing better than you ever have. This confidence makes for remarkable music making.

Now Stop Practicing!

It's recital time. It is also time to stop practicing.

Huh? *Stop practicing?*

I don't really mean that you should stop practicing for your recital. What I do mean is that you need to leave your other pieces behind. You need to stop working on the pieces that aren't going to be on the recital program. Set them aside, give them a break.

If you have been memorizing a pile of music over a long time, it is hard to stop that momentum. At some point you decided what is going to be on your recital program, and you need to focus only on that program. The program might include a couple of newly memorized works, and it will most likely include pieces you learned some time ago. Whatever the case, you need to let your in-process pieces take a break.

You might find that you are practicing less each day. No worry! You need to retain your focus and drive. By minimizing your work, you will maintain your interest in the program. Leave the learning time for when you don't have any immediate performances.

This is extremely hard for me to do. Before writing this chapter, I had a chamber music program to prepare in the midst of all of my summer memorizing work. Since I played the program before, I knew I would only need about two weeks to pull it together, including my own solo works. For a few days, I mapped out my usual practice and then tacked on the program. This added about an hour to my two-and-a-half hours of regular practice. When I had to meet with the violinist, I did my two-and-a-half *plus* my additional hour … *plus* two-and-a-half hours with her. By the end of the day, I was exhausted. Worse, I definitely didn't feel like practicing the next day. And my back hurt from all of that playing!

After that experience I realized I needed to be wiser about how I was using my time. This meant I had to drop my summer work in favor of preparing the recital. That was hard to do, especially with all of my momentum.

It is more fun to learn music than to perform it. A case in point, I had already prepared and performed the program with the same violinist, so there wasn't much learning to do. We just had to pull it together, and I, therefore, didn't want to drop my daily work.

Here is the perversity of the situation. Everything I do in the practice room is to bring my music to a performing level. When I get a chance to perform, however, it takes tremendous discipline to motivate myself to focus only on the performance. I am not alone in this sentiment.

This is the reason that, ever since I started playing from memory, I have accepted fewer and fewer "gigs." Gigs take up valuable practice time, and I am not in this for my own ubiquity. As I stated, we owe it to our audiences to be the best that we can be. Taking gigs for the sake of taking gigs doesn't help our own situation if we want to be musicians of the highest quality.

(I do understand, too, that many musicians must accept gigs for the sake of the money. This might be why the giggingmost musicians around don't play recitals. They gig. In spite of those circumstances, there continues to be a culture among musicians to take on more than they can handle, all for the sake of ubiquity or pole position on the call list. Ah, if only musicians practiced as much as they really should. Remember what I wrote about memorization forcing good habits?)

Whenever I find myself near a recital or even a practice performance, I have to go through the pain of cutting out my other work. This, in the end, makes my recital preparation more engaging and fun, especially since I am not cutting corners and trying to fit everything in. The end result is that I approach my recital time with a sense of confidence, relaxation, and the knowledge that I have given 100% to the preparation.

Practicing for Performance

I already posited that a piece and, in turn, a recital is never truly ready. There will always be room for improvement. The more we work at what we do, the more we are critical with what we do.

This is not to say that we shouldn't be working towards a goal of "ready to go." There is a point at which you have to decide that your interpretation and knowledge of a piece must crystallize for the sake of your performance. You don't want to go on stage with lingering doubts about your interpretation.

I tend to reach this crystallization stage about three or four weeks before a recital. Even if in doubt about the interpretation of a particular piece, I must stop *trying* to make it work, and I have to set my mind to making a convincing performance. Of course, at this stage, I already have a pretty solid interpretation, but sometimes I find that a tempo hasn't settled or that I still have some questions about rubato. Whatever the case, the experimentation must stop at this stage, because I need to be working on the performance—not the interpretation.

Here is an example: I am preparing a performance that is about three weeks away. I already played the program before, so I started a light review about five weeks before the concert. Last week I began seriously revisiting the program. Because of the program's length and complexity, I put all other repertoire on hold.

In returning to the program, I noticed some issues with tempi and interpretation. (Thankfully the memory retention has been quite solid.) In order to address those issues, I spent all of last week and this week focusing on the program in that capacity. Next week I need to start reigning in that corrective work and settle into a state of assuredness about my interpretations. The next time I prepare this particular recital, I will undoubtedly find new issues to address. It is always an uphill battle!

As I approach the recital (and the same could be said for practice recitals), I know that there isn't enough time in the day for me to go over every single piece with the same amount of detail. I would still like to touch on every piece every day, so I will develop a pattern of alternating types of work. A day might look like this:
- Pieces A, C, E, G, I: do mental work from landmarks with metronome.
- Pieces B, D, F, H, J: play slowly from landmarks with metronome; play at tempo with metronome; play without metronome.

I will alternate this pattern the following day so that I cover everything equally. As the recital approaches, I will try to stay off of the metronome for the at-tempo work so that I become more reliant upon my inner metronome. Likewise, I will keep up with the slow tempo work for the sake of technique. Most important throughout this entire process is the mental work. I never stop doing this. The mental practice is not only about memorization. It is also about confidence in interpretation.

Keep reassessing your daily practice goals. If you establish a routine, it is far too easy to let it become a habit instead of intelligent, thoughtful practice. To that end, don't forget to list your daily goals in your practice log while working towards total presence in your own practice. Your practice habits, including total presence, will manifest themselves on stage, so be wise.

More Mental Work

You have already included mental work as part of your daily routine, and you are using it in conjunction with your recital preparation. At this stage your mental work is primarily a reinforcement of your visual memory and landmarks, but it also reinforces your aural memory. By using a metronome, you have maintained a consistent, patient approach to the process of learning and confirming your work away from the instrument.

In the early stages of memorization, mental work is a large part of the learning process, while in the middle stage, use mental work to solidify landmarks and confirm what is being done at the instrument. By the performance stage, mental work should take on a new significance, requiring a new level of discipline.

Just as your work at the instrument shouldn't become routine, your mental work needs to remain fresh and focused. In the days before a recital, one can easily slip into a pattern of doing mental work with landmarks and then going to the instrument to play those landmarks or perform the program. What else can you do once you really know your landmarks? Should you just keep reviewing them?

When I feel that I know a program cold, the first thing to disappear is my concentration and total presence. In those situations I have no trouble playing through the program during my practice time. In fact, it is quite easy. Unfortunately I play it in a way that is lacking in focus or interest. It becomes too comfortable. Of course, once on stage, it becomes all too apparent that I haven't been practicing in a focused manner and have taken too much for granted. Panic can set in, and I start to realize that my home practice has been entirely unfocused, even though it felt very comfortable and secure. Performing brings everything into hyper-focus, and if we are not prepared for everything that might happen, disaster will strike.

To avoid a lack of focus in the days before a performance, set a slow metronomic tempo and mentally work through the program, not by landmark, but from start to finish, piece by piece. Although it is difficult to maintain concentration during this, the metronome will keep you on track. If you lose focus, back up a bit and pick up where you left off. Even if you don't make it to the instrument that day, you will feel good that you worked through the program in a thoughtful manner instead of just speeding through a thoughtless routine. This type of work will not only confirm your knowledge of the program, it will also serve to settle your mind into a concentrated and confident state when performing.

Practice Performances Redux

I already discussed practice performances in the context of playing a newly learned piece or two. Now with a recital on the horizon, you should be planning one or two practice performances of the entire recital. In the case of a few pieces, it is relatively easy to find a moment when you can play for someone or a small group. A full recital takes commitment, however, not just for you but for your practice audience as well.

As I wrote before, you want to make sure that your audience makes you nervous. To that end your practice recital should not be too casual, and it should strive to replicate the emotions present in a public recital. You can have a lot of fun and turn it into a nice event, as opposed to an academic exercise.

I am lucky to be able to use my home as a practice venue. I am even luckier that my wife is really into this. Not only can I tap into her guest list as well as my own, she also likes to plan a really great post-recital cocktail party. What is nice about her guest list is that it includes people I have never met before, and this keeps me on my toes. It is a blessing to have someone act as host so I can focus on what I am there to do. For my own house recitals, I print programs, set up formal seating (as formal as I can be), and plan an intermission. In other words, I try to make it as real as possible.

If you don't have a home venue, you can always rely on some old standbys: churches, other people's homes, or even nursing homes. Whatever venue you choose, however, it is important to let the audience know that you are playing a *practice* recital. This isn't to take the edge off of your nerves, but it is to let the audience know exactly why they are there. I mention this because, especially if you are playing in a church or nursing home, it is easy for some venues to appropriate your practice event into something bigger than what you intend it to be. Just be careful.

You need to be thoughtful about your audience. If performing locally, be careful that you don't siphon off your local audience by inviting them to your practice recital. In local cases I tend to invite people who I know are unable to attend the "real" recital. In addition, develop a rotating list of guests so that you aren't always inviting the same people every time. Otherwise they might get bored with you, *and* you will cease to be nervous with them.

Just as recommended for playing a few pieces, you can always use Google+ or another resource to stream your practice recital to the internet. You might not get a nice cocktail reception out of it, but it is an option when you have trouble coming up with an audience. Who knows? You might even build an internet following!

Hanging out Backstage

I already wrote a bit about what to do and what not to do right before a performance. Among my suggestions are:
- Don't play entire pieces before a performance. The distraction of nerves can make for memory slips, and then those slips will haunt you when you are playing the actual program.
- Don't review your entire program backstage. This practice invites self-doubt.
- Don't create a ritual of your backstage experience. What happens if you don't have enough time for your ritual? Does it mean that things won't go well?

So, don't play, and don't review. What are you supposed to do? Those green rooms can be dark and lonely places.
- Check a few things, such as tempi (with a metronome) and landmarks, but don't become obsessive about it.
- Breathe and relax while focusing positively on your upcoming performance. Visualize success. Meditation has a calming effect.

If you are not an advanced meditator, you can only do so much—and backstage time can be fairly lengthy. With that in mind, get your mind off the performance itself. Try to read. Play a game on your smartphone. Of course, always be aware of time so that you aren't caught off guard when it is time to go.

Backstage crew can be extremely poor people to talk to before a performance. (Remember the story about Charles Rosen and the Carter Sonata?) They are often uninterested in the concert, and they can be quite silly. Your backstage time should be used to clear your mind and your nerves, so even if you are trying to take your mind off of the performance, be careful how you do it.

Bring snacks and water for your time backstage, and always have something to eat at intermission, when you will need to replenish your energy. Bananas are known for their stress-reducing properties, so bring a couple. Because the stress of playing seems to dry out one's throat, make sure to have plenty of water on hand.

None of these suggestions are, of course, germane to the *memorized* performance, but, as memorization takes more focus than playing from score, it doesn't hurt to remind yourself of these good habits. In an ideal world, backstage time would be fun and exhilarating. More often than not, however, it isn't ... so be prepared!

Stage Presence

Once I returned to playing from memory, my on-stage needs changed, just as my backstage activities changed. When I performed with music, I was much more concerned with non-musical things, such as lighting, page turns, and bench height. Bench height is still important, but now the bench position is not forced by a need to see the music and therefore is not as important as it once was.

When performing from score, I did what I could to focus before playing, but because playing from score didn't force all of the good habits I have been writing about, I wasn't as concerned with some basic issues. Believe it or not, those basic issues included optimal tempo, listening to the room, and hearing a piece before playing it. Indeed, I had gotten quite used to just diving into the music. After all, I had the score to save me from any major accidents.

For me, the score became a barrier to the music. I don't just mean this metaphorically, but rather in the most concrete terms. I couldn't hear the instrument as well, and in turn, I wasn't listening to the way the music was sounding in the room. Ultimately this meant that I wasn't listening to the music.

Imagine: week after week of practice with a score in front of my nose, regularly not hearing the instrument at its best. No matter what you think about memorizing music, you certainly must agree this is an aural impediment.

(Obviously I am writing here specifically to keyboardists whose scores block direct sound from the vibrating strings. Doesn't a baffle—that is, a score—in front of other instruments affect the way the sound enters the room? A 'cello, a flute, a violin, a voice? I think so.)

Today I think before I play. I settle down before the keyboard, and I envision the opening measures of what I am about to play. I breathe, I calm myself. I pay close attention to finding my starting tempo. I recall my meditation practice in order to be totally present.

For this reason I think twice before agreeing to a lecture recital. It is very hard to settle into a state of total presence when wondering, "What did I just say?" or "What should I say?" A lot of presenters ask if I would talk about pieces before I play them. I only do this if I am *really* comfortable with a program, and I strongly discourage it for anyone who is just becoming comfortable with playing by heart.

Don't forget: presenters don't often have your best interest in mind. You can easily talk them down by saying that, as a memorizing musician, you need to stay focused. If they don't like it, they can hire the guy who needs a page turner!

The Importance of a Clear Mind

Once when giving a practice performance for a friend, I decided, as an experiment, not to meditate before playing. I had several reasons for this. First, I had already performed the program multiple times, and I wasn't particularly nervous about this practice performance. (This too-comfortable playing is something I generally discourage.) Second, I don't like superstitious rituals, and I wanted to see if meditation had become a ritual. I don't like the idea that things will go wrong if I don't force myself to do something pre-performance. Third, I really wanted to see what would happen if I didn't meditate.

Shortly before playing, my friend and I discussed fingering, and I talked about the difference between "strong" and "weak" fingers at the harpsichord. We talked about using weak fingers for ornamentation. And then I began the practice performance.

For the *entire* first half of the program, I kept thinking about our conversation! I focused on my fingering, my ornaments, and what I had just talked about with my friend. In other words, I was lacking in total presence, and at times, I was instead suffering from *total distraction*.

During my five minute intermission, I disappeared so that I *could* meditate, and as a result, the second half of the program was much more focused.

I don't care what you call it: meditation, clearing the mind, being alone. Whatever it is, I believe we must carefully cultivate our pre-performance minds. Not only should we strive to avoid thoughts that regularly plague us, but also we should keep ourselves from being distracted by whatever goes on backstage. Moreover, what we do on stage can also become a major distraction.

Keep the mind clear!

Resuscitating a Program

You have now performed your recital several times, and you have put the program to sleep for months or even years. Now you can get back to learning new music. The day will come, however, when you will want to resuscitate your pieces, most likely for a performance. How will you go about this?

While I think it is a good idea to have a piece or two always ready to play for people, it is not necessary to keep an entire program ready to go at all times. Not only does this constant readiness make for tedious work (and, hence, tedious performances), but also there is not enough time in the day to keep all of those balls in the air.

If you have done your memorization work well, bringing back repertoire shouldn't be much trouble at all. Sometimes when I revisit older pieces, however, I find that I didn't memorize them that well. This makes for extra work that I would rather not be doing just before a recital. This, again, is why it is so important to work from good habits.

In any case, I find that no matter what I bring back will require new work. Interpretation is not fixed, and your interpretation will change from the time you put a piece to sleep until you wake it up again. Your own memorization techniques and abilities will always be improving, so you might find that your process from just a few years ago differs from now.

Because of this I tend to wake up a previously played program about five or six weeks before a performance. This allows time to apply any new interpretive ideas while also giving me enough time to bring the program back to memory. At this point I am not practicing the program at full capacity; that won't happen till about two or three weeks before the performance. Some light practice is a good way to assess what has changed in my conception of the program and whether any memory and technical issues appear.

In the run-up to a revisited recital program, I return to the places in my practice log from the time I originally worked on the program. This reminds me of landmarks, metronome and optimal tempo markings, and practice skills for each piece. If I documented everything well, the resuscitation process is surprisingly fast, and it can be quite fun.

Good memorization practice should result in easy resuscitation down the road. That is yet another reason why I have been preaching patient learning.

Conclusions

A Summary of How

Writing a concluding summary to a book on memorization seems counterintuitive to the dynamic nature of memorization. There is always more that we can and should do.

Throughout this book, I keep coming back to some necessary elements:
- practice log
- timer
- metronome
- landmarks

As I wrote this book, I found that, while I had been using those elements consistently, my application of them was in continual need of refinement. At times I was sorely lacking in one of the most discipline-challenging parts of any memorization practice:

mental work away from the instrument.

In the coming days, months, and years, I shall continue to refine my approach to memorization. I don't ever think it will get easier, but I do think that I will get better at it. Will I memorize faster? I hope so, although another main concept of my approach is:

patience.

It is not about speed; it is about quality. This becomes especially apparent when returning to pieces put aside for some time.

Above all it is important to know that you and I will continue to find new memorization techniques along the way. These will be applied to what we are working on at the moment, and they will be applied to works that we are bringing back to life. Just as I improved from my early memory slip experiences, we can continue to improve further down the path.

There is always more to learn.

Postscript

Every so often I come upon a Gordon Ramsay cooking show on television. During his programs Ramsay repeatedly refers to chefs' *passions*. If a chef doesn't cook to a high standard, Ramsay will often ask if the chef has "lost his passion."

I have puzzled over the concept of "passion" for some time. What is passion? How does a lousy meal mean that a chef has "lost his passion?" Does Ramsay mean that the chef has lost a commitment to excellence?

The creation of this book has helped to define my passion. I have always been an avid practicer, but writing about my practice has made me realize the extent of my passion. Even more so, quantifying my daily practice with my practice log has shown me how much work I put into my passion. If passion is defined by quantity of work, I certainly have a lot of passion.

This, however, is not about quantity. It is about *quality*, and this book has influenced the quality of my practice time. I went from knowing (and writing about) what is good for me to consistently implementing what is good for me. If I had passion before I started this book, then it has increased tenfold.

We can always do whatever we do better, and we should always strive to improve what we do. For me, memorization was missing from my performing life, and I *knew* deep inside that I could do better. Is it "better" to play from memory? I think so, and I believe that audiences think so.

If you have passion for what you do, you will always refine that activity. Passion has forced me to work even harder at my performing. If you are passionate about what you do as a musician, you must always work harder.

What is your passion, and what are you doing about it?

Appendix I

This article originally appeared in the September 2011 edition of The Diapason. *(Reprinted with permission.)*

Dear Harpsichordists, Why Don't We Play from Memory?

Over the years, I've asked myself why harpsichordists aren't expected to memorize, and, like many harpsichordists, I'd been asked by audiences why I didn't play from memory. I know of many reasons! Memorization keeps the player from free ornamentation. It isn't historical. Bach is too hard to memorize. We're too busy with all of the continuo playing. The world's greatest harpsichordists don't memorize. But the best excuse of all is that *we don't have to*. This is a great excuse, and I've used it so many times that I even recommend it!

Last spring, I made a personal moratorium on playing solo repertoire from score. At that time, I anticipated a two-year hiatus from solo recitals. After all, I hadn't played a memorized program since 1995.

When I mentioned to a violinist colleague that I hadn't memorized in over fifteen years, she remarked, "What, you don't have repertoire worth memorizing?" The truth is, I'd spent a lot of time looking at B-list composers. Maybe there was something to what she was saying. Her comment immediately reminded me of a Dutch harpsichord builder who once said, when I asked him what could be done to advance the instrument, that the harpsichord would not survive if players did not begin to adhere to an industry standard of memorization. The violinist's comment also reminded me of a harpsichordist who said that he didn't own a metronome.

On one hand, we harpsichordists know that pianists and other instrumentalists have given us an industry standard. On the other hand, we want to be different from the conservatory mold and, hence, not own metronomes. We justify our counterculture with historical anecdotes and other excuses. But the fact remains that pianists—our closest relatives—would not have careers without memorized programs (and, I might add, metronomes).

Granted, harpsichordists come from different strains of the musical world. There are musicologists among us, and there are organists among us as well. There are also those who simply play for pleasure and others who really just enjoy continuo playing. But I am really writing to those who define themselves as concert harpsichordists and professors of harpsichord.

How did I arrive at my moratorium? Part of it was a sense that I never truly learned my programs. I was essentially reading music on stage, worried that the lighting was good enough or that I'd make my page turns in time or afraid that I'd lose my place in the score. Part of it was the lingering suspicion that the emperor had no clothes. I once played a solo piece from score for a Bach festival in which I was a featured soloist. My performance was followed by a high school violinist who played his solo partita from memory. What was my excuse for not taking the time to learn and perform the music from memory? But above all of the reasons for my moratorium, it is that I wanted to communicate better with my audience. Performing is about communication, and having my eyes glued to the music is not a good way to communicate.

As an undergraduate pianist, I played from memory. But then I switched to harpsichord as a major, and I was told not to memorize. Once, when I wanted to play part of a program from memory, my teacher suggested that I was being a show-off and that it was not in the spirit of the repertoire. A few years later, concerned about entering graduate school, I played my graduate auditions from memory. However, when I started my studies, my new teacher told me that I no longer had to play from memory. And I took the lazy, easy way out: I didn't.

Ultimately, I find it embarrassing that our colleges and conservatories are giving out degrees in harpsichord performance without a memorization component. How is it that pianists, for instance, are required to memorize programs—including works of Bach—but we don't have to? Of course: because *we don't have to*. Or could it be because professors of harpsichord themselves are not playing from memory?

Coming back to memory after many years began with some baby steps, including some serious, but recoverable, memory lapses. This season, I played a couple of memorized pieces on chamber music programs, and I've now graduated to a half-recital. I'll be at a full recital long before my two-year hiatus ends, especially now that I've realized that my ear, technique and theory comprehension are much better than they were years ago. Playing from memory has done some remarkable things for me. First, it puts good repertoire into direct focus. In other words, if you have to commit something to memory, what do you want to spend your time on? My phrasing has changed, and I've developed more personal interpretations through the internalization of the music. I no longer have to put up with page turns, poor lighting, small music desks and photocopies falling from the instrument.

My subjective experience will not convince other harpsichordists to memorize. And, considering that harpsichordists may still view themselves with some counterculture cache, the argument that pianists set an industry standard may not seem valid. But the harpsichord is no longer esoteric, and it is now—and has been for some time—a mainstream instrument. This is what we harpsichordists should all want: a larger audience and a public that embraces the instrument as a viable concert instrument. But there is a price to pay for this notoriety: our field has to grow up and do what is expected on the modern concert stage.

I am not writing this article to diminish the work of those who continue to play from score, and I submit this argument without any arrogance. Simply put, I am writing this as a plea for the future of our instrument. In order for the solo harpsichord to continue on the concert stage, it is imperative that the next generation of harpsichordists be expected to play from memory. Dear harpsichordists, I am not asking *you* to play from memory; I am asking you to require your students to play from memory. We need a sea change to meet the standard that is expected on the modern concert stage—because *we don't have to* is no longer an excuse.

Appendix II

A Checklist for Memorizing a New Piece

Beginning
- mark landmarks
- establish slow practice tempo

Early Stage
- Mental Work
    - one landmark with metronome at slow tempo
- Playing Work
    - play one landmark with metronome at slow tempo
    - play next landmark

Once all landmarks are learned
- Mental Work
    - review landmarks in reverse order with metronome at slow tempo
- Playing Work
    - play landmarks in reverse order with slow metronome at slow tempo
    - play through with metronome at slow or optimal tempo
- Perform
    - meditate five minutes and play through

Middle Stage
- Mental Work
    - keep reviewing landmarks in reverse order with metronome at slow tempo
- Playing Work (alternate as time allows)
    - play all landmarks with metronome at slow tempo
    - play through with metronome at optimal tempo
- Perform
    - meditate five minutes and play through till reaching a solid comfort level
    - schedule practice performance

Performance Stage
- Mental Work
    - straight through with metronome at slow tempo
- Playing work
    - play all landmarks with metronome at optimal tempo
- Perform
    - meditate five minutes and play piece

Appendix III

A Checklist for the Memorized Program

Beginning four to five weeks before performance
- Mental work
    - refresh memory of landmarks
    - work through landmarks in reverse order with metronome at slow tempo
- Playing work (alternate as time allows)
    - play all landmarks with metronome at slow tempo
    - play through with metronome at slow tempo

Beginning two weeks before performance
- Mental work
    - confirm all landmark starting points
    - work through landmarks in reverse order with metronome at slow tempo
- Playing work (alternate as time allows)
    - play all landmarks with metronome at slow tempo
    - play through with metronome at optimal tempo
- Perform
    - play through pieces every second or third day
    - schedule practice performance ahead of concert performance

Beginning three days before performance
- Mental work
    - straight through with metronome at slow tempo
- Playing work
    - play all landmarks with metronome at optimal tempo
- Perform
    - meditate five minutes and play program

INDEX

Aesop	21
A-list music	15, 52
anxiety	see "fear"
aural	16–18, 30–32, 34–37, 41–42, 47, 68, 72
B-list music	15, 81
Bach, J.S.	xiv, 4, 13–15, 27, 32, 81–83
backstage	57, 59–60, 71–72
Beethoven, Ludwig van	xiv
Bell, Larry Thomas	xiii–xv, 9
binary form	4, 14, 51
blog-to-book	1–2, 19–20
bringing back pieces	see "resuscitation"
Buddha	59
Carno, Zita	xiv
Carter, Elliot	9, 71
church service	53, 70
compassion	60
concerto	8, 15, 28, 33, 35, 57
conservatory	3, 15, 19, 35, 40, 82
Couperin, Louis	14
cultural climate	11

Dear Harpsichordists, Why Don't We Perform from Memory?
          5–6, 81–84

The Diapason	81
Doppelgänger	50
fear	5, 18, 22, 43, 53, 55–57, 60, 62, 82
fingering	7, 32, 34, 73
"for fun" playing	49

form and analysis	see "theory"
Gallwey, Timothy	57
gigs	65–66
good habits	7, 22, 24, 43, 48, 66, 72
Google+	54, 70
Greene, Barry	57
impatience	10, 13, 27, 32, 41, 45, 60, 64
improvisation	50, 52, 61–62
Inner Game	57–59
insomnia	6, 37, 41, 48
intonation	6
Juilliard School, The	xiv
landmarks	18, 26–28, 30–33, 36–37, 39, 41–42, 46, 48–51, 55–58, 61–62, 67–69, 71, 77, 86–89
leapfrogging	28, 48
Liszt, Franz	xiii
Longy, Renée	xv
Ma, Yo-Yo	xiv
meditation	48, 58–61, 68–69, 71, 73–74
memory slips	1–3, 8, 13–14, 22, 26, 28–29, 47, 49–52, 61–62, 68, 71, 83
memory types	see "aural," "tactile," or "visual"
Mendelssohn, Felix	xiii
mental practice	17–18, 21, 23, 33–34, 36–39, 42, 45–50, 57, 62, 68–69, 75, 86–89
metronome	7, 18–19, 22–24, 31, 36–38, 42, 48, 67–69, 71, 77, 81–82, 86-89
mnemonic	28–31, 33–34, 36–37, 55
Mozart, W. A.	xiii
optimal tempo	22–23, 38, 48, 72, 86–89
ostinato bass	32–33
passion	41, 78–79
patience	2, 13, 15–16, 21, 25, 27, 34, 43, 52, 60, 64, 75, 77
Persichetti, Vincent	xiv
Philippine Madrigal Singers	8
practice log	7, 15, 18–20, 24, 26, 46, 48, 58, 68, 77–78
practice performances	53–54, 56, 58, 63, 66, 69, 73, 86–89
Providence Journal	54
Ramsay, Gordon	78
recordings	30, 34–35, 38, 50
resuscitation	67, 74–75

Rephann, Richard	40
repetition	xiv, 4, 6, 17, 21, 31
ritornello	32–33
rondo form	14
Rosen, Charles	9, 71
Rubinstein, Arthur	40
Ruiz, Michael	19, 40
Saint-Saëns, Camille	xiii
Schumann, Clara	xiii
sentimental practice	23
Sessions, Roger	xiv
Skype	54
slow practice	6–7, 13, 23, 31, 34–35, 38, 42, 48, 69, 86–89
smartphone	21, 59, 71
solfège	xv
sonata form	33, 51
stopwatch	21
super-concentrated playing	49
tactile	16–18, 23–25, 30–32, 34, 37–38, 41, 47–49
theme and variation	14
theory	xiv, 26, 33, 51, 83
timer	15, 20–22, 24, 31, 46, 48, 59, 77
total presence	see "meditation"
Touching the Void	43
trap doors	51–52
Tristan und Isolde	xiv
"true" memorization	26
visual	16–18, 28–32, 34, 36–37, 41–42, 47–49, 56, 68
Whitelaw, John	50
Wikipedia	29–31, 50
Winkler, Allan	6
Yale University	40

Made in United States
Orlando, FL
19 September 2023